Embodied Cognition, Acting and Performance

In this collection of chapters, the four branches of radical cognitive science—embodied, embedded, enactive and ecological—dialogue with performance, with particular focus on post-cognitivist approaches to understanding the embodied mind-in-society; de-emphasising the computational and representational metaphors; and embracing new conceptualisations grounded on the dynamic interactions of 'brain, body and world'. In our collection, radical cognitive science reaches out to areas of scholarship also explored in the fields of performance practice and training as we facilitate a new inter- and transdisciplinary discourse in which to jointly share and explore common reactions of embodied approaches to the lived mind.

The chapters in this book were originally published as a special issue in *Connection Science*.

Experience Bryon, PhD, is Senior Lecturer at the Royal Central School of Speech and Drama, UK, specializing in Practice as Research and Interdisciplinary Performance. She is also author of *Integrative Performance: Practice and Theory for the Interdisciplinary Performer* (Routledge 2014) and *Performing Interdisciplinarity: Working Across Disciplinary Boundaries Through an Active Aesthetic* (Routledge 2018).

J. Mark Bishop is Professor of Cognitive Computing at Goldsmiths and Director of TCIDA (Tungsten Centre for Intelligent Data Analytics), UK. Mark also serves as a 'co-opted expert on Artificial Intelligence' for ICRAC (International Committee for Robot Arms Control).

Deirdre McLaughlin is a PhD candidate at the Royal Central School of Speech and Drama, UK. She has directed and performed in over 50 productions within the United States and United Kingdom with companies including Shakespeare's Globe, Battersea Arts Centre and National Theatre Studio. Her research interests include applications of cognitive science to the actor's process.

Jess Kaufman is practitioner-researcher in New York, USA, investigating experiences of meaning-making in audience responsive devising. She has been published in *Theatre and Performance Design* and *ArtsPraxis*, and her credits include Off-Broadway and US national tours. She gained her MA in Advanced Theatre Practice from the Royal Central School of Speech and Drama, UK.

Embodied Cognition, Acting and Performance

Edited by
Experience Bryon, J. Mark Bishop,
Deirdre McLaughlin and Jess Kaufman

Routledge
Taylor & Francis Group

LONDON AND NEW YORK

First published 2018
by Routledge

2 Park Square, Milton Park, Abingdon, Oxfordshire OX14 4RN
52 Vanderbilt Avenue, New York, NY 10017

Routledge is an imprint of the Taylor & Francis Group, an informa business

First issued in paperback 2019

British Library Cataloguing in Publication Data
A catalogue record for this book is available from the British Library

ISBN13: 978-0-8153-8576-9 (hbk)
ISBN13: 978-0-8153-8576-9 (pbk)

Typeset in MyriadPro
by diacriTech, chennai

Publisher's Note
The publisher accepts responsibility for any inconsistencies that may have arisen during the conversion of this book from journal articles to book chapters, namely the possible inclusion of journal terminology.

Disclaimer
Every effort has been made to contact copyright holders for their permission to reprint material in this book. The publishers would be grateful to hear from any copyright holder who is not here acknowledged and will undertake to rectify any errors or omissions in future editions of this book.

Contents

Citation Information

The chapters in this book were originally published in *Connection Science*, volume 29, issue 1 (2017). When citing this material, please use the original page numbering for each article, as follows:

Preface

Preface to the special issue: embodied cognition, acting and performance
Experience Bryon, J. Mark Bishop, Deirdre McLaughlin and Jess Kaufman
Connection Science, volume 29, issue 1 (2017) pp. 1

Chapter 1

Transdisciplinary and interdisciplinary exchanges between embodied cognition and performance practice: working across disciplines in a climate of divisive knowledge cultures
Experience Bryon
Connection Science, volume 29, issue 1 (2017) pp. 2–20

Chapter 2

Autopoiesis, creativity and dance
J. Mark Bishop and Mohammad M. al-Rifaie
Connection Science, volume 29, issue 1 (2017) pp. 21–35

Chapter 3

Embodiment: a cross-disciplinary provocation
Deirdre McLaughlin
Connection Science, volume 29, issue 1 (2017) pp. 36–42

Chapter 4

Stanislavsky's system as an enactive guide to embodied cognition?
Ysabel Clare
Connection Science, volume 29, issue 1 (2017) pp. 43–63

Chapter 5

Reverse engineering the human: artificial intelligence and acting theory
Donna Soto-Morettini
Connection Science, volume 29, issue 1 (2017) pp. 64–76

For any permission-related enquiries please visit:
http://www.tandfonline.com/page/help/permissions

Notes on Contributors

Mohammad M. al-Rifaie is a Lecturer at the Department of Computing, Goldsmiths, University of London, UK.

J. Mark Bishop is Professor of Cognitive Computing at Goldsmiths, University of London, UK, and Director of TCIDA (Tungsten Centre for Intelligent Data Analytics), UK. He also serves as a 'co-opted expert on Artificial Intelligence' for ICRAC (International Committee for Robot Arms Control).

Experience Bryon, PhD, is Senior Lecturer at the Royal Central School of Speech and Drama, UK, specializing in Practice as Research and Interdisciplinary Performance. She is also author of *Integrative Performance: Practice and Theory for the Interdisciplinary Performer* (Routledge 2014) and *Performing Interdisciplinarity: Working Across Disciplinary Boundaries Through an Active Aesthetic* (Routledge 2018).

Ysabel Clare is Associate Lecturer at the Department of Theatre and Performance, Goldsmiths, University of London, UK.

Shaun Gallagher is Lillian and Morrie Moss Chair of Excellence in Philosophy, University of Memphis, USA. He is also Professorial Fellow on the Faculty of Law, Humanities and the Arts at the University of Wollongong, Australia.

Pil Hansen is Assistant Professor at the School of Creative and Performing Arts, University of Calgary, Canada.

Jess Kaufman is practitioner-researcher in New York, USA, investigating experiences of meaning-making in audience responsive devising. She has been published in *Theatre and Performance Design* and *ArtsPraxis*, and her credits include Off-Broadway and US national tours. She gained her MA in Advanced Theatre Practice from the Royal Central School of Speech and Drama, UK.

Rick Kemp is a Professor and Head of Acting and Directing at the Department of Theater and Dance, Indiana University of Pennsylvania, USA.

Deirdre McLaughlin is a PhD candidate at the Royal Central School of Speech and Drama, UK. She has directed and performed in over 50 productions within the United States and United Kingdom with companies including Shakespeare's Globe, Battersea Arts Centre and National Theatre Studio. Her research interests include applications of cognitive science to the actor's process.

Robert J. Oxoby is Professor and Department Head at the Department of Economics, University of Calgary, Canada.

Donna Soto-Morettini is Senior Lecturer at the School of Arts and Creative Industries, Edinburgh Napier University, UK.

Preface to the special issue: embodied cognition, acting and performance

Experience Bryon, J. Mark Bishop, Deirdre McLaughlin and Jess Kaufman

This Special Issue of Connection Science was born of an interdisciplinary exercise that took place over the years of 2014–2016 as the Embodied Cognition, Acting and Performance Symposium, part of the annual AISB conference. In this journal you will find artists and scientists crossing the boundaries of their disciplines allowing for the emergence of new knowledges and practices.

The editorial team and symposium organisers include:

Prof J. Mark Bishop, Ph.D. is Director of TCIDA (the Tungsten Centre for Intelligent Data Analytics) and Professor of Cognitive Computing at Goldsmiths, University of London. Under the aegis of Cognitive Computing Mark's research spans Artificial Intelligence – its theory and applications – and the philosophy of Artificial Intelligence. Mark has published over 180 articles and 2 books, alongside running research projects attracting funding in excess of four million pounds.

Experience Bryon, Ph.D. is Senior Lecturer at Royal Central School of Speech and Drama specialising in Practice as Research and Interdisciplinary Performance. She is also author of *Integrative Performance: Practice and Theory for the Interdisciplinary Performer* (Routledge 2014) and the forthcoming *Performing Interdisciplinary: Working Across Disciplinary Boundaries Through an Active Aesthetic* (Routledge 2017).

Deirdre McLaughlin is currently a Ph.D. candidate at The Royal Central School of Speech & Drama, University of London and the Director of MA Acting at Arts Educational Schools London. Deirdre has directed and performed in over 50 productions within the US and UK with companies including Shakespeare's Globe, Battersea Arts Centre, and National Theatre Studio. Her research interests include applications of cognitive science to the actor's process.

Jessica Kaufman is a performance maker and researcher based in New York City with an MA in Advanced Theatre Practice from the Royal Central School of Speech and Drama. Her research praxis investigates ecological experiences of meaning-making in devised theatre for young audiences. She is co-author of "Infrasonic Tones in Theatrical Design" (*Theater and Performance Design*, Vol. 2, Routledge 2016).

The editors would like to thank:

Prof Tony Prescott, Editor-in-Chief, Connection Science and all the Taylor & Francis editorial team, for without whom which this special issue would not have been possible.

Transdisciplinary and interdisciplinary exchanges between embodied cognition and performance practice: working across disciplines in a climate of divisive knowledge cultures

Experience Bryon

ABSTRACT

Although Embodied Cognition and Performance Practice could be said to have in common that they live in the fields of hermeneutics and epistemology concurrently, and with this are interested in perception, knowledge, experience and agency without privileging any of them or presuming a linear or status relationship among them – there still remains a divisive disciplinary gulf. This paper provides a critical history of the science/humanities divide, exposing prejudices and practices that often impede productive interdisciplinary relationships between Cognitive Science and Performance, and offers suggestions forward towards a more productive middle field allowing for the possibility of new knowledge(s).

something a little more than a dashing metaphor, a good deal less than a cultural map. (C.P. Snow)

Forging the "Gulf"

The "something" in the above quote is the notion of the "Two Cultures" referred to in that (in)famous lecture which took place on 7 May 1959 in Cambridge titled "The Two Cultures and the Scientific Revolution". It set off "the mother of all academic shouting matches" (Gould, 2011, p. 89), concerning the tensions between what Snow called at the time "literary intellectuals" and "research scientists". After the lecture, Snow rightly stated that "Just as the concept of 'the two cultures' has been accepted, so has the existence of a *gulf* between them" (Emphasis Added) (Snow, 1960, p. 217).

At the time, science as a discipline was still largely flying on the coattails of the great advances in seventeenth century Europe:

> a brief, and sufficiently accurate description of the intellectual life of the European races during the succeeding two centuries and a quarter up to our own times is that they have been living upon the accumulated capital of ideas provided for them by the genius of the seventeenth century. (Whitehead, 1967, p. 39)

Today, although the scholarly, political, disciplinary and funding landscapes have slightly altered and, with this, the naming of the "two" territories, there still remains a perceived "gulf" between the Sciences and other enterprises of knowledge production, despite a flurry of interdisciplinary activity in recent years. The Embodied Cognition and Performance Practice Symposium, for which this Special Edition of Connection Science is an outcome, is one example. It became evident during the Symposium that both Embodied Cognition and Performance Practice are concurrently hermeneutic and epistemological. They are both interested in the practice, reception and perception of knowledge, action, agency and experience, and in their enquiries do not necessarily privilege or presume a linear or status relationship between these. However, even with this in common there is still work to be done, assumptions to question and institutional prejudices to confront to better negotiate the historic "gulf".

As we work towards rigorous and valuable interdisciplinary exchanges between Embodied Cognition and Performance Practice, this article will sit in the discomfort of this "gulf", review embedded prejudices and often fatuous arguments between and within the two cultures, reveal the ways these have trickled down and influenced Performance Practice and Embodied Cognition and, hopefully, offer some clarity and ways forward, allowing for the emergence of new knowledges born of our exchanges.

Although the history of Snow's lecture, with its subsequent criticism, could be dismissed as a thing of the past and contained as an out of touch elitist conversation held within an Oxbridge parochialist privileged landscape, it is still within us and in our institutions, influencing decisions on policy, funding, career progression, project approvals and publication. In order to understand how we got here, appreciating that Snow's notion of "two cultures" presaged the even more contentious premises behind what would later be called the "Science Wars" is useful.

The martial metaphor here is a little annoying, as there were no battles, no winners or losers, or, most importantly, few if any "practicing" participants from either side fighting, really. However, as it is it was quite a tiff. Following Snow's lecture, the "gulf" grew and arguments extended across the pond, drawing from European philosophical influences and creating much contention in the US. Postmodern thinking began to gain traction, and with this came a social, linguistic and cultural analysis of a "pure" science, critically reviewing its ideological underpinnings.

Within the 10 years following Snow's lecture, the student uprisings in France disturbed modernist ideology and confronted political doctrine, historic materialism and social reality. Complex socio-cultural networks were recognised while established modernist hierarchies dissipated. This was a time ripe for the birth of interdisciplinary scholarship, but also of great resistance. The "Science Wars" and other such debates established newly minted categories on both sides of the "gulf".

German Social theorist Wolf Lepenies' statement exemplifies the type of stance that got things so heated:

> Science must no longer give the impression it represents a faithful reflection of reality. What it is, rather, is a cultural system, and it exhibits to us an alienated interest-determined image of reality specific to a definite time and place. (Collini, 1998, p. 1)

Those perceived to agree with such sentiments were painted as living within an "academic leftist" camp comprised of humanists, social scientists and radical feminists. With the emergence of the interdiscipline cultural studies, there came a blurring of boundaries, with an augmented interest in cross-disciplinary activity among the humanities and sciences. It was in this climate that Performance Studies, along with Science and Technology Studies (STS), which will be discussed in the next section, was born. Many considered this a serious threat, articulated most succinctly by Lyotard when he introduced the notion that interdisciplinarity erodes disciplinary authority (Lyotard, 1984). As I have argued in past publications, however, "How can we erode what we do not know, what we have not practiced, and what is not embodied?" (Bryon, 2009, p. 136). Regardless, the fear was real and played out in interesting ways, laying the foundations for our current interdisciplinary climate.

Gross and Levitt, self-identified scientific realists, were aggressive defenders against any view of science that favoured social context over pure logic of argument. For them, this cross-disciplinary trend was akin to an intellectual nihilism. (I will discuss in the next section that because Performance Practice had no such defenders against this trend, there were no "performance wars")

> Many notable historians and sociologists of science have long held misgivings about intellectual nihilism that offers itself as "cultural constructivism"; but they have been reluctant to challenge it for fear of gaining a reputation as sissies, too weak-kneed to play the exhilarating game of "epistemological chicken. (Gross & Levitt, 1998, p. xiii)

This game of "epistemological chicken" was played dirty, but to great effect in the controversial stunt perpetrated by physics professor Alan Sokal. Inspired by Gross and Levitt's take that the academic left as being "permeated by jargon, philosophical dogma, and political attitudes drawn from the world of postmodern literary criticism" (Gross & Levitt, 1998, p. 81) and their pointed statement:

> The notion of "cultural critic," in its postmodern form, embraces a certain kind of sociologist as well as a certain kind of literary scholar. They publish in the same journals and appear at the same symposia, speaking the same language and sharing the same attitudes. (Gross & Levitt, 1998, p. 81)

Sokal successfully submitted a nonsensical article titled "Transgressing the Boundaries: Towards a Transformative Hermeneutics of Quantum Gravity" (Sokal, 1994) in which he posited that quantum gravity was a social and linguistic construct. It was published in the journal *Social Text* in its spring/summer edition in 1996. For many it proved that the leftist, postmodern, subjective and relativist humanities was an incestuous, non-rigourous melting pot of pretentious mumbo-jumbo. In reality it proved that *Social Text* had not yet put in place a proper peer review process, and as such no physicist had read the paper prior to its acceptance. But the damage was done.

In John Gray's highly provocative account of human nature, *Straw dogs: Thoughts on human and other animals*, an account of knowledge that arguably eats its own tail, he perpetuates the above mentioned "gulf" to the point of condemning humanity as a solipsistic exercise largely perpetrated by notions of misplaced belief.

> Outside of science, progress is simply a myth. In some readers of *Straw Dogs* this observation seems to have produced a moral panic. Surely, they ask, no one can question the central article of faith of liberal societies? Without it, will we not despair? Like trembling Victorians terrified of losing their faith, these humanists cling to the moth-eaten brocade of progressive hope. Today religious believers are more free-thinking. Driven to the margins of a culture in which science claims authority over all of human knowledge, they have had to cultivate a capacity for doubt.

In contrast, secular believers – held fast by the conventional wisdom of the time – are in the grip of unexamined dogmas. (Gray, 2002, p. xi)

What we often find within discussions such as these is a perpetuation of "two cultures", albeit in different terms. The "gulf" now is no longer articulated as in Snow's divide between "literary intellectuals" and "research scientists". Of course many historic readings, plotting a path from the "Science Wars" of late last century to the beginning of the new, may easily and correctly plot a different path citing different moments; however, I think we can agree that Christensen's summarisation of Gray's two-sided assessment articulates a fair estimation of where we are arguably stalled, especially when we fail to engage productively across disciplines.

> Gray adopts a very peculiar position in an on-going and often contentious academic debate that pits scientific realists on the one hand against social constructivists on the other. At stake in this debate is the very nature of science: for scientific realists, science proceeds by discovering and verifying empirical realities; for social constructivists, science proceeds by inventing a plausible means of interpreting nature and then persuading colleagues and the general public to believe in it. (Christensen, 2005, p. 2)

With this, new lines were drawn between science and the humanities, with the scientists often regarded as positivists rather than relativists, naturalists rather than humanists, realists rather than constructivists, empirical thinkers relying on logic and evidence rather than interpreters valuing aesthetics, with proper science on the side of falsifiable truth and New Age pseudo-science on the other; and with this also a peculiar political penchant to label the Humanities category as Leftist, with science on the Right. This entire set of dualisms and generalisations, not excluding the aforementioned "weak-kneed sissies and trembling Victorians", is, ironically, a perfect example of the type of socially constructed reality created by those that so ardently fought to eradicate it. Interestingly, even Sokal, after drawing so strongly from Gross and Levitt with the epithet "right wing", had to clarify – however, only in a footnote.

> In this footnote I have also engaged in the habit – followed ritually throughout the essay – of tagging Gross and Levitt with the epithet "right wing". Of course, this epithet is inaccurate: Gross is a curmudeonly old-fashioned liberal and Levitt is a member of the Democratic Socialists of America. But even if Gross and Levitt *were* hard-core right-wingers, how would that affect the validity or invalidity of their arguments? (Sokal, 2008, p. 28)

Regardless of the story told and the drama played out, the stuff of the "Science Wars" worked quite effectively towards the assumption that science lives on more properly on the side of epistemology, with the humanities on the side of hermeneutics. However, when it played out . . . it was not so simple.

The problem with the "*Studies*"

Both Performance Studies and STS emerged from ideas expounded around the late 1970s in the same climate in which the aforementioned Cultural Studies emerged, a climate where cultural Critic and Anthropologist Clifford Geertz shared approaches to social thought surrounding behaviour in his often cited article *Blurred genres: The refiguration of social thought* in American Scholar, Spring 1980 (Geertz, 1980). Jackson identifies Geertz's notions of "game", "drama" and "text" within the context of ritual and human behaviour as a grounding influence. Through Geertz, who "came to symbolize 'anthropology' for a generation of non-anthropologists, wax[ing] eloquent about the blurring, particularizing, and analogising of social thought, the discipline of performance studies secured an institutional hold" (Jackson, 2004, p. 147) – as did the discipline of STS.

As there are entire sets of books, departments, and critical histories that are devoted to defining and re-positioning the evolving nature of these interdisciplines, of course within this small section of this particular article there is a limit to what can be covered; however, what I aim to illustrate is the ways in which these "studies" as disciplines differ in status and function in relation to the practices from which they draw and also influence.

STS takes a variety of anti-essentialist positions, with a scepticism of the natural as an essential custodian of knowledge with inherent properties that contain truths. The field investigates how scientific knowledge and technological artefacts are *constructed*. Sismondo summarises:

> The source of knowledge and artifacts are complex and various: there is no privileged scientific method that can translate nature into knowledge, and no technological method that can translate knowledge into artifacts. In addition, the interpretations of knowledge and artifacts are complex and various; claims, theories, facts, and objects may have very different meanings to different audiences. For STS then, science and technology are active processes, and should be studied as such. (Sismondo, 2010, p. 11)

According to prospectus of the STS Graduate Program at Vancouver British Columbia, topics for study within a STS programme will generally include such things as how laboratories work, how to understand the development of scientific practices and technological objects in social context, examination of the ethics of science and technology, analysis of expertise and the authority of science in democracies, understanding relations between science and public policy, and exploring representations of science and technology (University of British Columbia, 2016).

At the core of this social-constructivist approach to science is the notion that scientists, with their network of technologies, artefacts and ideas within an institutional culture, and operating within dynamics of social interactions, *construct* truth and facts rather than discover, find or uncover them.

Where STS seriously differs from the story of Performance Studies, however, is in the appropriation of its findings, vocabularies and contextualisations of its practices.

> Many, or even most, people who are involved in producing scientific knowledge and new technologies do not subscribe to the story that STS tells. For them, science is a progressive neutral activity that produces true knowledge and facts about the natural world through application of a standard method. Most scientists do not think that the knowledge they produce is contingent on social factors or conditions, only that it is constrained by the limits of scientific possibility, material and technical resources, of funding. (Erickson, 2005, p. 2)

This may be because within the scholarly institutional framework the standard account of formal science still holds a privileged position. "The standard account of formal science describes a project for science (the discovery of facts about the natural world), and prescribes a method – what we can call formal scientific method – by which this should be carried out" (Erickson, 2005, p. 54). Formal science rarely competes with STS for funding or status, and for the most part relies on different vocabularies and skillsets. STS has not re-defined the research languages or institutional parameters and modes of evaluation of formal science, although it can influence framings of these. Formal science is still more recognised than STS within academia. The same cannot be said for Performance Studies and the practices which they draw on within scholarly contexts. The practice of science has not been as compromised by becoming an *object of study* as the practice of performance when Performance became an object of study.

Performance Studies and its accompanying theories are often erroneously thought to offer critical articulations of Performance Practice. This is not necessarily so. Performance Studies has a direct heritage from the aforementioned branch of interdisciplines that was previously, derogatorily, referred to as coming from the "academic left". It is greatly influenced by poststructuralism and postmodernism, and has roots in literary theory and anthropology, with discursive criss-crossings in areas concerned with meaning, language, ritual, identity, society, behaviour and culture. For a more detailed comparative analysis of the development of Performance Studies and its key tenets, including *performativity* and *liminality*, see my previous publication *Integrative performance: practice and theory for the interdisciplinary performer* 2014, Chapter 2. In it, I concluded that the fact that Performance Studies has roots in social sciences and literary theory is significant to the way in which performance has come to be defined. It has also presented some problems with respect to how performance practitioners are characterised. "It is particularly of interest when looking at how our *way* of practice is often pulled away from subtle understandings of process, and instead categorised as a performative object that is embedded or positioned in the construction of a performance" (Bryon, 2014, p. 38).

Performance as a general term can be understood as a theatrical form, practice or event, such as a play, an opera, a piece of musical theatre or a dance; however, within Performance Studies everything that *does*, or is *done onto* and/or generates *meaning* can be seen as performance, and therefore used as a way to create hermeneutic readings and representations while examining theories of reception and repetition across many events, texts and/or identities. As one of the founding scholars of the discipline defined *performance*, or arguably un-defined it:

> One cannot determine what "is" a performance without referring to specific cultural circumstances. There is nothing inherent in an action in itself that makes it a performance or disqualifies it from being a performance ... every action is a performance ... What "is" or "is not" performance does not depend on an event in itself but on how that event is received and placed. (Schechner, 2002, pp. 30–31)

So when one *practices* performance with this definition, what is the practice exactly? With STS, the practice of science, even if put under a microscope, still maintains some sense of stability. However, as mentioned above, many *practitioners* of science do not need to adopt nor articulate their actions through the critical lenses of the theories expounded by STS to be deemed rigorous in scholarly contexts. This is not so for the performance practitioner when engaging in Practice as Research (for instance) at the postgraduate level. This is attributable partly to the unfortunate received divide that will be addressed further on, between those that do and those that think, the conservatoire artist and the university scholar, the artist and the analyser. Another, more recent definition, a little less strictly attached to the original anthropology and literary theory roots of Performance Studies:

> Performance is both a practice and a mode of analysis. It is a communicative behaviour for which there is no other name (that's to say, if you can call it acting you treat it as acting). It is a mode of analysis that works by framing, thinking of, its material as if it were performed, which is to say as if it were a deliberate communicative practice. (Shepherd, 2016, pp. 222–223)

This of course is true; however, this definition does not speak to that type of practice that is purposefully not communicating that practice at the core of Performance Practice that must precede communication: the scales, the barre work, the way of being in the doing of the doing so that one is in the flow of process, the act of the act – although, if looked at from the outside as an object of study, it like anything else could be seen to "communicate" – but being in the practice of the act is the practice of many performance practitioners, not the looking at it as an object.

I will argue later that the practice of a doing and the doing of a practice become a potential shared space where Embodied Cognition and Performance Practice engage in a mode of enquiry. I will also propose that this offers unprecedented possibilities for emergent knowledges about the human condition, especially if we do not fall into the modes of observation that derive from critical lenses that trap process as object before we can engage in the uncomfortable places of process and practice. Practice as/based/and Research can offer some models, but until both sides get inside of the thing, more rigorous interdisciplinary exchanges could be difficult. For Performance Studies some recognise this problem, as Conquergood attests to, but there has yet to be a satisfactory arrangement.

> A performance studies agenda should collapse this divide and revitalize the connections between artistic accomplishment, analysis, and articulations with communities; between practical knowledge (knowing how), propositional knowledge (knowing that), and political savvy (knowing who, when, and where). This epistemological connection between creativity, critique, and civic engagement is mutually replenishing, and pedagogically powerful. ... The ongoing challenge of performance studies is to refuse and supercede this deeply entrenched division of labor, apartheid of knowledges, that plays out inside the academy as the difference between thinking and doing, interpreting and making, conceptualizing and creating. (Conquergood, 2002, p. 153)

Unlike STS, what Performance Studies takes from Performance Practice is profound and what it gives back is difficult and negligible. In the linking all performative meaning to linguistic metaphors it often dilutes or bypasses the very things that make the *way* practice, rather than the *what* or *situ* of a practice of value. Importantly, STS remains a distinct exercise from that of empirical science practices. These are not funded from the same pots, neither are they evaluated as scholarship in the same manner. Performance Practice, having never experienced "performance wars" akin to the science wars, has not been given the same treatment. Within many Liberal Arts departments in the US and university/conservatoire hybrid institutional models in the UK, practice has been largely subsumed by the rhetoric of Performance Studies, bending to its critical discourse, evaluations of rigor and funding models, especially where interdisciplinary exchanges are concerned and where practice is explored as scholarship.

Science and performance – equal validity?

Paul Boghossian, author of Fear of Knowledge: Against Relativism and Constructionism, argues against what he terms *Equal Validity*, which he defines as a radically counterintuitive doctrine, a doctrine that posits that "There are many radically different, yet 'equally valid' ways of knowing the world, with science being just one of them" (Boghossian, 2006, p. 2). To illustrate his concerns he discusses American prehistory and cites a 1996 New York

Times Article titled *Indian tribes' creationists Thwart archeologists*. He discusses a dissonance between the scientific consensus, proven through archaeological findings, that humans first entered the Americas from Asia, crossing the Bering Strait around 10,000 years ago, and a Native American creation myth which tells the story of a people who emerged from within the earth as descendants of the buffalo people after supernatural spirits prepared the world for human kind. This concerns him because:

> ... we have a variety of techniques and methods – observation, logic, inference to the best explanation and so forth, but not tea leaf-reading or crystal ball-gazing – that we take to be only legitimate ways of forming rational beliefs on the subject. These methods – the methods characteristic of what we call science but which also characterize ordinary modes of knowledge-seeking – have led us to the view that the first Americans came from Asia across the Bering Strait ... For this sort of deference to science to be right, however scientific knowledge had better *be* privileged – it had better not be the case that there are many other, radically different yet equal ways of knowing the world, with science being just one of them. (Boghossian, 2006, pp. 4–5)

This idea seems to really disturb him and he further speaks to the notions of *credibility* and the problem with seeing Zuni creationism in line with archaeology and evolution in line with Christian creationism.

> Equal validity, then is a doctrine of considerable significance, and not just within the confines of the ivory tower. If the vast numbers of scholars in the humanities and social sciences who subscribe to it are right, we are not merely making a philosophical mistake of interest to a small number of specialists in the theory of knowledge; we have fundamentally misconceived the principles by which society ought to be organized. (Boghossian, 2006, pp. 4–5)

Despite the fact that one could spend an entire article unpacking the many difficulties here, including the equating of crystal ball reading with the people of the Lakota tribe, unfortunately this will have to wait for another time. Staying on point, the comparing an active disorganisation of society with "the ivory tower", evoking the leftist intellectual camp discussed earlier, has a certain hypocrisy, as the creationism story generally touted by the right (which he touches on only briefly, fluffing over this) could be seen as the same play with different props.

However, the most important point to be made here is the idea that Equal Validity is even a thing. Perhaps this is the wrong conversation, especially when it comes to fostering productive and rigorous scholarly environments able to allow for the emergence of new knowledges. Is "equal" so important? Equal to what exactly? Why not just different? And is something not made valid only by its own terms and culture, and with this, its discrete modes of evaluation?

Nelson, pioneer of Practice as Research and as such committed to "creative cross overs in an interconnected academy" which includes arts research that "demonstrates a rigour equivalent to that of the sciences", argues for a "both-and" type of epistemological space which includes "a more fluid 'knowing' ... " which might be located on the spectrum between types of knowledge rather than on the reverse side of an impervious 'knowledge/not knowledge' binary" (Nelson, 2013, pp. 23 & 39).

In order for us to foster a healthy and productive interdisciplinary environment between Cognitive Science and Performance, an approach like Nelson's may be more advantageous. However, it is not so simple, as there are legacies of prejudices that linger, even with the best of interdisciplinary intentions.

> In order to think critically about science, one must understand it at a reasonably deep level. This task, if honestly approached, requires much time and labor. In fact it is best started when one is young. It is scarcely compatible with the style of education and training that nurtures the average humanist, irrespective of his or her political inclinations. (Gross & Levitt, 1998, p. 5)

As discussed in the previous section, the *practices* within Performance Studies do not equate to the practice(s) that performance practitioners undergo and continue throughout their entire careers, day in and day out. Interestingly, the very type of exactitude, early training, rigour and commitment intimated by Gross and Levitt's somewhat insulting comment above is absolutely required of the ballet dancer, the opera singer and the actor, for instance.

The notion that performance practitioners are not able to engage or interested in engaging in theory and scholarly enquiry can also be misguiding. Pavis states: "Theory must be guided with real epistemological and methodological care. The crisis of academic research, particularly historical and dramaturgical research, probably stems from the sad conclusion that it doesn't seem to interest theatre people" (Pavis, 2001, p. 156). Here he expressed an ongoing perceived divide between what Jackson so eloquently describes as "She-Who-Is-Preoccupied-With-Making-Meaning" and "He-Who-is-Preoccupied-with-Meaning" (Jackson, 2004, p. 111). However, with the advent of Practice as Research PhDs and the increasing interdisciplinary projects being undertaken in the last decade, this perceived dualism is slowing being challenged. Further, William Newell, Executive Director of the Association for Integrative Studies at the Miami University of Ohio writes:

> While the notion that interdisciplinarians study complex systems tends to resonate well with natural and social scientists, it tends to sound strange (even alien) to humanists, not to mention those in the fine and performing arts for whom anything systematic is anathema . . . . The humanities and arts are more concerned with behavior that is idiosyncratic, unique, and personal – not regular, predictable, and lawful. If the natural and social sciences focus on the rules that govern behavior, the arts and humanities focus on the exceptions to those rules. Systems thinking seems more relevant to the practical, real-world problem solving of the sciences than to the probing and expression of meaning by humanists. (Newell, 2001, pp. 3–4)

Perhaps the physical theatre circus performer, the dancer who is practicing catches, the actor who needs to repeat systematic feats of emotional availability night after night and the opera singer reaching consistent high Cs might know a little about the necessity of regular, predictable and lawful, systematic analysis and practices born of the complex system of the emotive breath/body. In fact very often it is a serious matter of health and safety. Here we enter into misunderstandings about the values and operations to do with embodied knowledge, especially as activated within Performance Practice(s).

When Bruce McConachie, an influential advocate for interdisciplinary exchanges between theatre and cognitive science, examines the reasons why *our discipline* (for which one can only assume he means generally *theatre*) came late to cognitive science, he situates the argument within the aforementioned dualistic categories of theatre scholars as being humanists and relativists and scientists as naturalists and empiricists, one I have argued above lies more within the scope of Performance Studies rather than Performance Practice. He maintains that "scholars in our discipline remain committed to one or another area of poststructuralist theory, an orientation to knowledge that does not recognize the value of empirical science for humanistic investigation" (McConachie, 2013, p. 5).

While I appreciate the point, one does not necessarily preclude the other as a way of investigating the practice of doing theatre. As a PhD supervisor for some years now, I have seen various critical lenses being applied to the understanding of Performance Practice concurrently. I offer but one such example when I draw equally from the poststructuralist notion of performativity, next to phenomenology and cognitive science, to explore the notion of *self* in action as a performance practitioner (Bryon, 2014, pp. 9–20).

It is interesting when McConachie rests on the notion of falsifiability:

> By falsifying provisional theories, constructing alternatives, and searching for evidence to support them, scientists gradually forge new possibilities that offer more robust explanations ... Scientists do not arrive at objective truth, but, through experimentation and argumentation, good science narrows the range of possible explanations and interpretations. (McConachie, 2008, p. 9)

This statement has much merit, especially if we are discussing Performance Studies; however, one could certainly argue that performance practitioners experiment and establish clear processes and feedback as to what works, what is repeatable and what is physically emotionally feasible, narrowing the range of what is possible. Further, within the pedagogies and practices that are born as part of their experimentation, knowledge emerges that has as part of the discipline a necessity for clear interpretations and articulations of the ways one enacts practice as a doing. This is not so much a hermeneutic exercise as an epistemological one.

Regardless, in taking a more critical look at the all-encompassing notion of falsifiability as the validator of science over humanities, upon inspection things are not as cut and dried as one might have assumed.

The standard account of Science rests on the premise that "science is a form of knowledge that produces facts and fact-like statements" and with this tenet it "conflates science and knowledge, seeing them as indivisible" (Erickson, 2005, p. 55). The logical positivists of the Vienna Circle in the 1920s started with the notion of *verification*, which posits that

> ... a theory is proposed and the theory makes predictions that can be tested through observation. Scientists will skeptically adopt a theory, and will then test the theory by making observations. As the observations that confirm the theory accumulate, the theory achieves a scientific status. (Erickson, 2005, p. 56)

Karl Popper took things a step further with *falsification*, a theory of logic that despite seeming critical of the work of the Vienna Circle worked to fortify their logical positivist account of the world. He posited that experiments and observations are not there to *verify* but rather to *falsify* theories, and that if and until they are proved false, they are considered true. But what happens when we fail as an institution and society to test past theories and/or even try to repeat experiments that have entered the lexicon as scientific fact?

Recently, Brian Nosek's Reproducibility Project included 270 scientists repeating 100 published psychological experiments. The reproducible results were surprisingly low, with only about a third of the experiments able to be repeated effectively. This problem, however, is not just within psychology:

> There exists very little evidence to provide reproducibility estimates for scientific fields, though some empirically informed estimates are disquieting (Ioannidis, 2005). When independent researchers tried to replicate dozens of important independent studies on cancer, women's health, and cardiovascular disease, only 25% of their replication studies confirmed the original

result (Prinz, Schlange, & Asadullah, 2011). In a similar investigation, Begley and Ellis (2012) reported a meager 11% replication rate. (Nosek, 2012, p. 657)

There are many thoughts about this, which go from the unlikely case of outright fraud to the more likely ideas such as "publication bias", the thought that journals prefer to report positive results, and of course the fact that funding is not given generally to prove something wrong, especially when the positive result serves pharmaceutical companies and institutional profiles.

> Considering its central importance, one might expect replication to be a prominent part of scientific practice. It is not (Collins, 1985; Reid, Soley, & Wimmer, 1981; Schmidt, 2009). An important reason for this is that scientists have strong incentives to introduce new ideas but weak incentives to confirm the validity of old ideas (Nosek, Spies, & Motyl, 2012). Innovative findings produce rewards of publication, employment, and tenure; replicated findings produce a shrug. (Nosek, 2012, p. 657)

Reproducibility could be seen to live in the field of process and practice, a *way* of doing, rather than what or how was done. Performance practitioners operate and are valued in this active field constantly. Sadly, they often actually lose value when they fail to reproduce that high note, that extension of the leg or that ability to embody a character six nights a week with matinees on Saturday. Further, one can be both a scholar and a practitioner; one can move between making meaning and an interest in meaning and discovering knowledge. In fact, one of the things that Embodied Cognition and Performance Practice have in common is that they are both hermeneutic and epistemological concurrently, and with this interested in perception and knowledge without privileging either or presuming a linear or status relationship between the multifaceted aspects.

Problematics of interdisciplinary scholarship between the sciences and performance practice

Barthes was not wrong when he stated that interdisciplinarity is "not the calm of an easy security; it begins effectively (as opposed to a mere expression of a pious wish) when solidarity of the old disciplines breaks down". And with this he refers to an "epistemological slide", opposing this to an all important "break":

> He did not want to suggest some conscious decision to re-ground theory on a new foundation. Instead he sought to challenge the very notion of *foundation* through the event of structure. Once one takes the idea of structure seriously, one has to recognise that knowledge and learning are the effects of movements that are not within the realms of decision and knowledge. (Bryon, 2009, pp. 139–140)

The institutional *realms* of *this decision and knowledge* that I refer to in the above quoted previous article are determined in the ways we measure, support and evaluate knowledge and knowledge production. The British Academy's 2016 Report *Crossing paths: Interdisciplinary institutions, careers, education and applications* recognises this problematic, but also encourages researchers to engage across disciplines only *after* establishing themselves in an "academic home":

> We recommend that researchers should aim to develop an academic home, a secure base from which to carry out IDR. An academic home consists in those critical elements that allow researchers to build a career, including expertise in core methods; a set of publications within a

disciplinary area; ability to teach core courses in a discipline; and professional networks forged by attendance at conferences. (British Academy, 2016, p. 3)

This gets complex when the models of evidencing knowledge and the processes of knowledge production live within completely different aesthetics, vocabularies and ways of documenting/capturing evaluable outcomes across disciplines. In my forthcoming book *Performing interdisciplinarity: Working across disciplines through an active aesthetic* (Bryon, in press), I will argue that disciplines are not the custodians of knowledge, but that knowledge is an active process often born of the crossing and colliding of disciplinary concerns. Further, the need for a solid establishment within an "academic home", which customarily is situated within a home discipline which may not recognise modes of knowledge production from *other* disciplines, becomes particularly difficult for reasons discussed throughout this entire article, especially when crossing the humanities/sciences divide. The report recognises this to some extent.

> Evaluation is key to many of the barriers to pursuing IDR. Many of the reasons for avoiding inter-disciplinary projects relate to the fact that it is harder to publish outputs; such work is perceived to have less value to hiring and promotion panels; and one is less likely to be selected for submission to REF. However, none of these barriers is an essential aspect of IDR and they can be addressed by better and more appropriate evaluation. (British Academy, 2016, p. 4)

What constitutes better and more appropriate evaluation across the sciences and humanities has yet to be determined, and despite recognition that interdisciplinary exchanges offer productive spaces for innovation and impact, HE institutions and government, at the most basic of levels, perhaps unknowingly, impede this type of work systematically. The Stern Report (an independent review of the last cycle of UK-based research evaluation exercises) reveals a sense that interdisciplinary work has been disadvantaged through disciplinary "silos", which we can safely assume are directly correlative with disciplinary constructs.

> . . . interdisciplinary work was often regarded less favourably than mono-disciplinary research. Such perceptions may have contributed to the relative underrepresentation of interdisciplinary outputs in RAE / REF compared with the known proportion of such work revealed by other bibliometric surveys of UK interdisciplinary research. In contrast the interdisciplinary contributions to impact case studies featured strongly. (Stern, 2016, p. 15)

The Stern report states that despite the British Academy's aforementioned report, which identified the essential role of interdisciplinary research in addressing complex problems and research questions posed by global social, economic, ecological and political challenges, " . . . There is a concern that institutions were risk averse in submitting interdisciplinary work. We think that it is vital that interdisciplinary work is submitted, assessed and rewarded through the REF . . . " (Stern, 2016, p. 28)

When it comes to interdisciplinary exchanges between the sciences and performance, it is worth remembering that "The concept of humanities research as discovering new perspectives, or new information, is actually a very recent formulation", an aspect of the issue that Frayling so clearly pointed out. In addition, "prior to the turn of the century the word [Research] predated the division of knowledge into arts and sciences" (Frayling, 1993, p. 4).

Even the best intended efforts to highlight the value of non-scientific research can arguably create a bigger "gulf". Not wishing to pick on any one advocate, but rather to offer a publicly accepted example of a common approach: when Senator Kim Carr, Northern

Australia's Minister at the time for Innovation, Industry, Science and Research, said of the creative arts: "We should support these disciplines because they give us pleasure, knowledge, meaning, and inspiration. No other pay-off is required" (Carr, 2008), he represented a position that has long existed and does not necessarily help the situation. To say that the arts, especially when engaged in as part of scholarship and research, should merely be permitted to exist because they give a different sort of "pleasure, knowledge, meaning, and inspiration" is undermining. This gives the impression that it is difficult to measure rigour in the arts, and although this may be the case within select conditions earlier expressed in the section of this article on Performance and Science and Technological Studies, it is not the case when it comes to Performance Practice. Such reasoning also perpetuates the previously mentioned misperception of the arts living solely on the side of subjective meaning making and hermeneutics, with the sciences on the side of objective knowledge production and epistemology.

When the 1998 Australian Strand Report tried to address "a way forward as agreed by the academic creative arts community, by which government and institutions could address inequities and marginalisation within their respective spheres of operation", similar problems occurred. As Wilson points out, in the "years since its release only limited progress has been made and many of the same concerns remain". This may be because it is not really understood what the nature of this inequity is. She proposes that:

> The creative arts should be recognized not because of their similarity or equivalence with the prevailing disciplinary powerbase, but for their contribution to the furtherance of knowledge in their own fields and their value to Australian society as a whole (Wilson, 2011, p. 75).

This would certainly go some way towards solving the problem; however, it still remains that even though we are getting better at evaluating within our own fields, when we cross fields challenges are still present.

Although things are slowly changing, when we do see science and performance exchanges, it is usual to see the performance being used to *illustrate* as a way to make the sciences more understandable to the general public – and it is not unusual to see the sciences used in general terms to *validate* a discrete aspect of a performance-based enquiry. As further interdisciplinary research between Embodied Cognition and Performance Practice is engaged with, hopefully in part inspired by the Symposium of Embodied Cognition and Performance Practice that has taken place over the last three years as part of the Artificial Intelligence and Simulation of Behavior conferences in the UK, we see moves towards braver and riskier approaches that exceed the mere *illustration/validation* relationship. However, taking into account the current cultures of evaluation so tied into career progression, one can understand the caution.

Pitfalls and possibilities within inter/transdisciplinary exchanges between embodied cognition and performance practice

Dreaming forward to a day when interdisciplinary exchanges meet modes of evaluation that can properly assess and support truly innovative cross-disciplinary breakthroughs between the sciences and performance, it is a good time to take stock and consider the possible natures of exchanges between Embodied Cognition and Performance Practice. In order to stay ahead of the game, we not only need to have a better understanding of the provocative histories between the sciences and humanities, along with the difficulties surrounding institutional support and scholarly evaluations of interdisciplinary exchanges; we need also to look to possible ambiguities within our own camps.

Cognitive science (which Graff refers to as cognitive studies, interchangeably) is of course an interdiscipline in its own right and in being so presents an interesting conundrum.

> More than most interdisciplines, cognitive studies is distinguished by its many academic homes and attachments: a sign of both its potential and its limits. Its quest to become an interdisciplinary discipline across disciplinary clusters conflicts with opportunities to develop and become established as an interdiscipline. (Graff, 2015, pp. 17–18)

Embodied Cognition, aptly referred to as "research program – rather than a well defined theory", or separate discipline (Shapiro, 2011, p. 2) is an ongoing enquiry within cognitive science that is unified by a hunch that "cognitive processes are deeply rooted in the body's interactions with the world" (Wilson, 2002, p. 625). As part of the Embodied Cognition Symposium of recent years, of which this special edition of Connection Science is a result, we invited Performance Practitioners and Embodied Cognition researchers to engage across the 4 E's: embodied, embedded, enactive and ecological movements of research that are grounded in the dynamic interactions of brain, body and world. I will not review the 4 E's here, as this would take a book, and there are many great sources out there that refer to these, although sometimes within slightly different categories to highlight different arguments to do with efficacy (Shapiro, 2011; Wheeler, 2014; Wilson, 2002); however, for the purposes of this article the implications of this grouping is interesting.

Embodied Cognition, like Performance Practice, shares a problem of *seriousness*. Where Performance Practice, as discussed in the previous section, has the problem of being either misunderstood and/or misappropriated, and certainly mis-evaluated as scholarship when judged simply within the hermeneutic-based theoretical constructs of Performance Studies, Embodied Cognition comes under a certain level of suspicion when its enquiries are placed against the more traditional computational and representational models of Cognitive Science, with their embedded ontological commitments drawing from the aforementioned "standard account of Science".

Whilst for strong proponents, such as Varela, Thompson, and Rosch (1991), Thompson (2004) and Hutto and Myin (2013), the embodied approach is seen as a radical departure from standard Cognitive Science; which, as Adams wryly observes ".. is sweeping the planet" (2010, p. 619), for others perhaps hedging their bets, the jury is still out.

> Empirical findings support substantive versions of both the embedded and embodied theses. Yet, although these empirical findings reflect important trends in experimental design and in the modeling of cognitive processes, the theoretical import of such findings has been substantially oversold. (Rupert, 2009, p.242)

Rupert states that the embedded and embodied approaches offer little reason for the revision of computation and representation, and further that they do not represent the revolution against computationalist cognitive science but rather offer "friendly supplements to the orthodox view, not departures from it" and, importantly, that

> We have no reason to think cognition extends into the environment, and insofar as embedded and embodied go, it appears that we face more of a nudging than a coup. (Rupert, 2009, p. 242)

Wheeler stresses a certain conservatism, nodding to Shapiro's stance that "the methods and ontological commitments of standard cognitive science win out because of their proven track record" (Shapiro, 2014, p. 6) with a fairly strong criticism of the Phenomenological approach so often drawn on to varying degrees by performance practitioner/researchers when speaking from the notion of a sense-making body:

> In sum, the account of relevance-sensitivity on offer from the perspective of Merleau-Pontian, sense- making embodiment may well be revolutionary (non-representational, non- computational) in its implications, but it is dangerously incomplete, because it fails to deliver a compelling causal explanation of the phenomenon at issue. Indeed, the shortfall here is serious enough that one might wonder whether it constitutes a genuine advance over the representationalist alternative. (Wheeler, 2014, p. 381)

So here we have a good example of the type of interdisciplinary conundrum that occurs across disciplines, one that brings up the difficulties of working across different modes of enquiry and methods of knowledge production that are built on different methodological, hermeneutic, epistemological positions and grounded in different ontological commitments.

Phenomenology, of course, is not about causation; in phenomenology, "subjects and objects are essentially interrelated, a fact which any adequate account of subjects and objects must preserve" (Howarth, 2005, p. 791). Further, "Phenomenological accounts of subjects emphasize action and the body; accounts of objects emphasize the significance they have for us" (Howarth, 2005, p. 791). One of the reasons performance practitioner researchers are so attracted to it is because although proponents of phenomenology such as Husserl, Heidegger, Sartre and Merleau-Ponty et al. interpret the field differently, they share a thought enquiry that reveals "a method of philosophical investigation which results in a radical ontological revision of Cartesian Dualism" (Howarth, 2005, p. 791). Simply using a phenomenological account to explain things is not likely to match well within the empirical methods of measurement, explanation or evaluation born from the standard account of Science. However, drawing from such non-linear perspectives could offer alternative entries into the scientific enquiries, especially as we explore inter/transdisciplinary exchanges across Embodied cognition and Performance Practice.

When we work on putting various disciplines, practices and/or critical frameworks together, assessing them by any of the "one cultures" discrete model may not work. When discussing the problematics of interdisciplinarity, Moran, in reviewing Bennington's (Bennington, 1999, p. 104) astute critique of the prefix "inter" as *ambiguous* (as it can both be seen as a joining such as in "international" and as a separating such as in "interval"), observes:

> This ambiguity is partly reflected in the forging connections across the different disciplines; but it can also mean establishing a kind of *undisciplined space* in the interstices between disciplines, or even attempting to transcend disciplinary boundaries altogether. (emphasis added) (Moran, 2010, p. 14)

An undisciplined space may not need to be non-rigourous, especially as new knowledge emerges that exceeds the model and methods of the old evaluative measures. The notion of transdisciplinarity sits at the heart of this. When Nicolesu designated categories of disciplinarity he defined disciplinarity as one practice concerned with itself, as opposed to multidisciplinarity, a relationship which transgresses disciplinary boundaries while its goal remains limited to within the framework of disciplinary research. For him, "interdisciplinarity transgresses the boundaries of disciplines while its goal still remains within the framework of disciplinary research. Interdisciplinarity even has the capacity to generate new disciplines, like quantum cosmology and chaos theory" – not to mention research programmes such as Embodied Cognition. As a somewhat utopian vision, transdisciplinarity "concerns itself with what is between the disciplines, across the different disciplines, and beyond all disciplines. Its goal is the understanding of the present world, of which one of the imperatives is the unity of knowledge" (Nicolescu, 2005, pp. 143–144). McGregor, speaking of transdisciplinarity, offers that a " … complicated problem is hard to solve because it is intricate and detailed. A complex problem has the additional feature of emergence, the process of deriving some new coherent structures, patterns and properties" (McGregor, 2004). When we try to evaluate and/or fit the languages, skill sets, processes and practices of different disciplines from and into one another before giving time to work within the *undisciplined space* for a while, this is not complex or rigorous, but complicated and un-rigourous.

It may be useful to recognise the heritages that both Performance Practice and Embodied Cognition carry with them as different strands of "two cultures", the humanities and the sciences, and also to recognise the ways in which they depart from the "studies", whether they be that of performance or science, within which they are often critically situated.

As explained earlier, performance practice is not born of Performance Studies, and as such does not live exclusively or even mostly in the realm of representation and hermeneutic enquiry. It is in the practice of the practice where various techniques happen, as process in a mutually interdependent dynamic between brain, body and world; further, this is where the practitioner as self and the act as performance are made simultaneously as an emergent property of an act of doing. The practitioner therefore works/practices from inside/between as process. In my previous book I refer to this as the field of *performing* (Bryon, 2014).

> *Performance* may be a work of choreography, a play or a score. It can also be an exercise, executed in the classroom or practice studio, such as barre work, scales or sensory work. A performance can even be a doing or a verb, when that doing becomes the object. (We have all made the act of singing, dancing and acting a thing to tackle. This often happens in practice or in a lesson.) Performance is an outcome of you, the artist, doing something in a certain way. We will learn that when you try to do an outcome directly you leave the way of *Performing* and change that desired outcome. In short, we work under the understanding that we are *performer* (self), *performing* (way of doing) *performance* (what's done). (Bryon, 2014, p. 11)

I posit that performer does not do a performance, rather a performer does *something*, a practice of a practice, within a field called-*performing*. It is within this middle field, *performing,* that the practice of the practice, the doing of the doing occurs, and through that act of doing, both the Performer and the Performance emerge. The field of *performing* collapses the subject/object paradigm required from representational and hermeneutic-based theoretical underpinnings of Performance Studies. It is not linear. It is not representative. It is not causal. The dynamics that occur within the field of *performing* are part of an *active aesthetic*, a term that designates a processual space that precedes representation and is also self-reflective. It is a theory born from an interdisciplinary enquiry around performance *practice*, not Performance Studies.

Knowing that there is a serious difference between the "performance" of performance studies and the performance of the practitioner might be really useful going forward. Both Embodied Cognition and Performance Practice live in seriously dynamic places, but are also in danger of being pinned down by each other in ways that derive from the prejudices they have both encountered. Ironically, Performance Practice could be seen to be the more empirically solid of the two, with repeatable, testable and rigorous outcomes and Embodied Cognition could be seen to be a little subjective and interpretive. To achieve the type of innovation and the possibility of new emergent knowledge that I suspect those of us interested in this exchange feel is impending, we need to exceed the two-culture habit mentioned earlier of validation/illustration and enter a different understanding, perhaps not unlike Moran's notion of the "uncontainable real":

> In its constant search for the uncontainable "real", interdisciplinarity can disrupt the deceptive smoothness and fluency of the disciplines, questioning their status as conveyors of disinterested knowledge by pointing to the problematic nature of all the claims to scientific objectivity and neutrality. (Moran, 2010, p. 180)

Moving forward, perhaps performance practitioner/researchers may need to draw on Embodied Cognition for more than proof against a perceived Cartesian dualism as a simple justification of our experience, that the mind and body and world are connected in measurable ways within the practices of our practice. Embodied Cognition may need to distinguish between Performance and its Practice(s) to go deeper, exploiting the ways in which practitioners work from inside the act of doing, with no dissonance between the dynamics of witnessing the act of doing, serving/acting as representational elements, and being in a flow of doing.

Engagements between Embodied Cognition and Performance Practice have the potential to achieve emergent knowledge that could be deemed truly transdisciplinary. What might happen if we were to recognise our historic baggage and allow a *rigourous undisciplined space* to explore an *uncontainable* "real" that exceeds the mere aforementioned illustration/justification relationship between science and the arts, which unfortunately keeps us within the same old "two cultures" distinctions? If we are brave and rigorous, and work across disciplinary boundaries by engaging the *practices* of the disciplines rather than an *object* of discipline as a mere custodian of knowledge, we may allow for the emergence of new knowledges that resolve that thorny issue of two cultures: "something a little more than a dashing metaphor and a good deal less than a cultural map" (Snow, 1998, p. 217)

Disclosure statement

No potential conflict of interest was reported by the author.

References

Adams, F. (2010). Embodied cognition. *Phenomenology and the Cognitive Science, 9*, 619–628.

Begley, C. G., & Ellis, L. M. (2012). Drug development: Raise standards for preclinical cancer research. *Nature, 483*(7391), 531–533.

Bennington, G. (1999). Inter. In M. McQuillan, G. MacDonald, R. Purves, & S. Thomson (Eds.), *Post-theory: New directions in criticism* (pp. 103–119). Edinburgh: Edinburgh University Press.

Boghossian, P. (2006). *Fear of knowledge: Against relativism and constructivism*. Oxford: Oxford University Press.

British Academy. (2016). *Crossing paths: Interdisciplinary institutions, careers, education and applications*. Retrieved August 20, 2016, from http://www.britac.ac.uk/sites/default/files/Crossing 20Paths20-20Executive20Summary.pdf

Bryon, E. (in press). *Performing interdisciplinarity: Working across disciplines through an active aesthetic*. Oxon: Routledge.

Bryon, E. R. (2009). Experience interdisciplinarity and embodied knowledge: Towards an active aesthetic using integrative performance practice. In *Tanz im Musiktheater – Tanz als Musiktheater. Beziehungen von Tanz und Musik im Theater. Bericht über ein internationales Symposion, Hannover 2006* (pp. 135–146). Würzberg: Königshausen & Neumann.

Bryon, E. R. (2014). *Integrative performance: Practice and theory for the integrative performer.* Oxon: Routledge.

Carr, K. (2008). *The art of innovation: Address to the national press club.* Retrieved August 22, 2016, from http://archive.industry.gov.au/ministerarchive2011/carr/Speeches/Pages/THEARTOFINNOVATION -ADDRESSTOTHENATIONALPRESSCLUB.html

Christensen, B. (2005). *The problematics of a social constructivist approach to science.* In CLCWeb Vol 7.3.1. Retrieved from http://docs.lib.purdue.edu/clcweb/vol7/iss3/1

Collini, S. (1998). Introduction. In C. P. Snow (Ed.), *The two cultures (canto classics)* (pp. vii–1xxiii). Cambridge: Cambridge University Press.

Collins, H. M. (1985). *Changing order.* London: Sage.

Conquergood, D. (2002). Performance studies, interventions and radical research. In the drama review 46, 2 (T174), Summer. New York University and the Massachusetts Institute of Technology. 145–153.

Erickson, M. (2005). *Science, culture and society: Understanding science in the twenty-first century.* Cambridge: Polity Press.

Frayling, C. (1993). Research in art and design. *Royal College Research Papers, 1*(1), 1–5.

Geertz, C. (1980). Blurred genres: The refiguration of social thought. *American Scholar, 49*(2), Springer. 165–179.

Gould, S. J. (2011). *The Hedgehog, The Fox and the Magister's Pox: Mending the Gap between science and the humanities.* Cambridge, MA: Harvard University Press.

Graff, H. J. (2015). *Undisciplining knowledge: Interdisciplinarity in the twentieth century.* Baltimore, MD: Johns Hopkins University Press.

Gray, J. (2002). *Straw dogs: Thoughts on humans and other animals.* London: Granta Books.

Gross, P. R., & Levitt, N. (1998). *Higher superstition: The academic left and its quarrels with science.* Baltimore, MD: John Hopkins University Press.

Howarth, J. (2005). Epistemic issues in phenomenology. In E. Craig (Ed.), *The shorter Routledge encyclopedia of philosophy* (p. 791). Oxon: Routledge.

Hutto, D., & Myin, E. (2013). *Radicalising enactivism: Basic minds without content.* Cambridge, MA: The MIT Press.

Ioannidis, J. P. A. (2005). *Why most published research findings are false.* Retrieved August 16, 2016, from http://journals.plos.org/plosmedicine/article?id = 10.1371/journal.pmed.0020124.

Jackson, S. (2004). *Professing performance, theatre in the academy form philology to performativity.* Cambridge: Cambridge University Press.

Lyotard, J.-F. (1984). *The post modern condition: A report on knowledge.* (G. Geoff Bennington & B. Massumi, Trans.). Minneapolis: University of Minnesota Press.

McConachie, B. (2008). *Engaging audiences: A cognitive approach to spectating in the theatre.* London: Palgrave MacMillan.

McConachie, B. (2013). *Theatre & mind.* London: Palgrave Macmillan.

McGregor, S. L. T. (2004). *The nature of transdisciplinary research and practice.* http://www.kon.org/ hswp/archive/transdiscipl.pdf

Moran, J. (2010). *Interdisciplinarity.* Oxon: Routledge.

Nelson, R. (2013). *Practice as research in the arts: Principles, protocols, pedagogies, resistances.* Basingstoke: Palgrave Macmillan.

Newell, W. H. (2001). A theory of interdisciplinary studies. *Issues in Integrative Studies, 19,* 1–25.

Nicolescu, B. (2005). *Transdisciplinarity – past, present and future.* Paper presented at the second world congress of transdisciplinarity: What education for sustainable development? Attitude – Research – Action. Vitoria/Vila Velha Brazil.

Nosek, B. (2012). An open, large-scale, collaborative effort to estimate the reproducibility of psychological science. *Perspectives on Psychological Science, 7*(6) 657–660. Sage Publications.

EMBODIED COGNITION, ACTING AND PERFORMANCE

Nosek, B. A., Spies, J. R., & Motyl, M. (2012). Scientific Utopia: *II. Restructuring incentives and practices to promote truth over publishability. Perspectives on Psychological Science, 7,* 615–631.

Pavis, P. (2001). Theatre studies and interdisciplinarity. *Theatre Research International, 26,* 153–163.

Prinz, F., Schlange, T., & Asadullah, K. (2011). Believe it or not: How much can we rely on published data on potential drug targets? *Nature Reviews Drug Discovery, 10,* 712–713. doi:10.1038/nrd3439-c1

Reid, L. N., Soley, L. C., Wimmer, R. D. (1981). Replication in advertising research: 1977, 1978, 1979. *Journal of Advertising, 10,* 3–13. doi:10.1016/S0149-2063_03_00024-2

Rupert, R. D. (2009). *Cognitive systems and the extended mind.* New York, NY: Oxford University Press.

Schechner, R. (2002). *Performance studies, an introduction.* New York, NY: Routledge.

Schmidt, S. (2009). Shall we really do it again? The powerful concept of replication is neglected in the social sciences. *Review of General Psychology, 13,* 90–100. doi:10.1037/a0015108

Shapiro, L. (2011). *Embodied cognition.* Oxon: Routledge.

Shapiro, L. (2014). *The Routledge handbook of embodied cognition.* Oxon: Routledge.

Shepherd, S. (2016). *Performance theory.* Cambridge: Cambridge University Press.

Sismondo, S. (2010). *An introduction to science and technology studies.* Chichester: Wiley-Blackwell.

Snow, C. P. (1960). Afterthoughts on the "Two cultures" controversy. In *Encounters: An anthology from the first ten years of encounter magazine* (pp. 216–225). New York: Basic Books.

Snow, C. P. (1998). *The two cultures (Canto classics).* Cambridge: Cambridge University Press.

Sokal, A. (2008). *Beyond the hoax: Science, philosophy and culture.* Oxford: Oxford University Press.

Sokal, A. D. (1994). Transgressing the boundaries: Toward a transformative hermeneutics of quantum gravity. *Social Text, 46/47,* 217–252. Retreived from http://www.physics.nyu.edu/faculty/sokal/transgress_v2/transgress_v2_singlefile.html

Stern, L. N. (2016). *Building on success and learning from experience: An independent review of the research excellence framework.* Retrieved August 13, 2016, from https://www.gov.uk/government/uploads/system/uploads/attachment_data/file/541338/ind-16-9-ref-stern-review.pdf

Thompson, E. (2004). *Mind in life: Biology, phenomenology and the sciences of mind.* Cambridge, MA: Harvard University Press.

University of British Columbia. (2016). *Science and technology studies.* Retrieved August 12, 2016, from https://sts.arts.ubc.ca

Varela, F. J., Thompson, E., & Rosch, E. (1991). *The embodied mind: Cognitive science and human experience.* Cambridge, MA: MIT Press.

Wheeler, M. (2014). Revolution, reform, or business as usual? The future prospects for embodied cognition. In L. Shapiro (Ed.), *The Routledge handbook of embodied cognition* (pp. 374–383). Oxon: Routledge.

Whitehead, A. N. (1967). *Science and the modern world: Lowell lectures 1925.* New York, NY: The Free Press.

Wilson, J. (2011). Creative arts research: A long path to acceptance. *Australian Universities' Review, 53*(2), 68–76.

Wilson, M. (2002). Six views of embodied cognition. *Psychonomic Bulletin and Review 9*(4), 625–636.

Autopoiesis, creativity and dance

J. Mark Bishop and Mohammad M. al-Rifaie

ABSTRACT

For many years three key aspects of creative processes have been glossed over by theorists eager to avoid the mystery of consciousness and instead embrace an implicitly more formal, computational vision: autonomy, phenomenality and the temporally embedded and bounded nature of creative processes. In this paper we will discuss autopoiesis and creativity; an alternative metaphor which we suggest offers new insight into these long overlooked aspects of the creative processes in humans and the machine, and examine the metaphor in the context of dance choreography.

1. Introduction

And how will you enquire Socrates, into that which you know not? What will you put forth as the subject of your enquiry? And if you find what you want, how will you ever know that this was the thing that you did not know? (Plato, "The Meno", circa 380bc)

Although, perhaps surprisingly, the term "creativity" has a relatively youthful etymology – it was as recently as 1927 that Alfred North Whitehead first coined the term in his Gifford lectures at the University of Edinburgh, (later published as "Process and Reality" Whitehead, 1929), a term now so ubiquitous, that its recent origin is obscured – people have been contemplating the process of creation for millennia: from Plato in "The Meno" (Whitehead 1929); through nineteenth-century and early-twentieth-century theorists whose accounts reified its conscious, almost divine, nature (e.g. by Wallas 1926 who explicitly engaged with its lived, phenomenological component; for Wallas *intimation* is the feeling a creative person gets when a solution is on its way and *illumination* the point at which the creative idea bursts forth into conscious awareness); to the modern era where the computational zeitgeist has encouraged purely formal accounts, more amenable to mechanical instantiation and explanations.

In contrast, in this paper we resist the computational turn and instead argue for a *lived*, phenomenological account of creativity, predicated on a *strong* notion of the embedded, embodied mind and enactivism (Varela, Thompson, & Rosch, 1991). An account that takes seriously the idea that creative processes:

(1) have a conscious, phenomenal element – it feels like something "to create" and "to know";

Figure 1. Pina Bausch watching her young dancers parade in a new production of *Kontakthof* ("Dancing Dreams", (c) Real Fiction 2010).

(2) are temporarily bounded;
(3) abound with notions such as, "embodied flow" " being in the zone", etc. which typically entail an altered mode of "being in the world" – neither fully subjective nor objective: the potter at his wheel; the mathematician lost in her equations; the tennis player enmeshed in a long, hard rally.

In this context we wish to rehabilitate older notions of creativity (such as that from Wallas 1926) – which engage with the subjective (feeling of creation) and also invoke another state of being (neither fully objective of subjective) – in a new enactivist account delineated by Varela et al. (1991), in terms of Maurice Merleau-Ponty's "entre-deux":

> The world is inseparable from the subject, but a subject which is nothing but a project of the world; and the subject is inseparable from the world but a world which is nothing but a project of the subject.

In Figure 1 we see the iconic German dance choreographer, Pina Bausch, as she leads 40 teenagers, who have never heard of her or her work, into a new production of perhaps her most minimalist Tanztheater, *Kontakthof*. How, given the times that she has staged the piece since its inception 1978, did she succeed in bring-forth something new?

We believe that a clue to the answer may lie in the very processes Bausch used in re-staging *Kontakthof*. Her work with the 40 teenagers was not merely a re-staging of set choreography (which often means the dancer mimics, learns or copies, rather than *interprets*[1]), but a more *organic* improvisational process, specific to Bauschs own creative process of re-staging around pre-existing choreography, for which interpretation and learning of the movement gestures goes hand-in-hand.

2. Creativity in movement and dance

There are many ways to think about systems that choreograph movements that we socially conceive of as dance. This theoretical work [2] is inspired by Alfred North Whitehead's *process view of organisation*[3] (Whitehead 1929), viewed though the transformational conceptual-lens of *autopoietic theory* (Maturana & Varela, 1973); according to which we view a creative system as a clearly delineated and identifiable network of *continuously operational* component producing processes and concomitant elements, bounded as an autonomous entity *within its own creative environment*.

So construed, the autopoietic dancer can never be fully satisfied with her work, but continually re-engages a complex process of "attention" (on *her* current movement context) and "reconstitution" (of *her* body), as she *creatively* reflects and *enacts* her world.

The autopoietic dancer lives in a universe of *meaning-distinctions* – the totality of which constituting her *dance-field* – and her dance begins as creative processes are drawn to, and collectively attend, these distinction(s); from which, at successive instants, she chooses one element, the most "interesting" gesture, to (re)interpret. In this manner, the autopoietic dancer continuously reflects and refracts back into the world, *she* has just brought forth, reinventing her universe in order that she may subsequently generate further new (re)interpretations.

As interpretations disappear with their appearance, they cannot be altered, but only give cause for the production of new movements, which are subject to the same mechanism. Thus, while there is a stimulating "dance-field" with which to interact – *and she continues to (re)interpret interesting and meaningful gestures* – this autopoietic unity will continue intact. Conversely, as the dance-field becomes less stimulating, the meaning-distinctions become less interesting and the autopoietic unity more-likely to fade and ultimately dissolve; in the very moment of such movements coming into being, they already fade away and the dancer returns to reflect stillness again.[4]

3. On "meaning distinctions" and the "dance-field"

Central to the operation of the dancer's autopoietic unity is the identification of interesting meaning distinctions in the dance-field which, through her dance, she is able to (re)interpret.

3.1. Relationship to the Stanislavsky system

Under the gaze of the "autopoietic dancer", we conceive of her dance-field as comprised of "meaning distinctions" emerging from the dancer's umwelt [5] of elements and gestures – *an open door; a movement of the head; the tension in a finger or arm; an inviting smile; a light; a memory invoked; a shadow, etc.* – in this manner "meaning distinctions" of most interest to the dancer, neither fully subjective or objective in character, are brought-forth through her choreographic interaction with the environment.

The totality of such "atomic" meaning distinctions – delineating her sensorium, *or field*, of movement embedded in sight, sound, touch and personal lived history – comprise the artist's *dance-field*. By modulating the distinctions, she is drawn to attend, as she creatively interacts with and explores her environment, the autopoietic dancer adapts what she construes as [artistically] "meaningful" in her own historical dialogue.

Furthermore, by analogy with what one scholar of Stanislavsky calls the "attention field" Clare (in press), the "dance-field", so defined, has a strong resonance with core ideas from Stanislavsky; as Clare (in press) observes:

> The arrangement of information in Stanislavskys inner world, then, is orientational, or adpositional, because it is orientated in positional relationships to a source in a notional three-dimensional space. In an adpositional model relationship is key. Therefore, in this perceptual model, the circumstances of a persons life at any given moment (on-line) are located perceptually in space, adpositionally: around the body. At any moment, we are experiencing a particular configuration of available thoughts, memories, and feelings: I have called this an *attention-field*. Patterns and consistencies within this field are apparent to the observer as that information is leaked both verbally and non-verbally.

3.2. Relationship to dynamic field theory

In modern cognitive science, *Dynamic Field Theory* outlines a important shift towards a new and intentionally integrated theory of cognition. Thus, in their introduction to the work of the DFT Research Group, as they move towards a unified theory of cognitive dynamics, Spencer and Schoner suggest:

> DFT provides an embodied account, that is, neural processes are grounded in sensory and motor processes that are anchored on a body situated in a physical environment ... we are pursuing a general theory that spans perception, action, and cognition ... carrying forward a set of common principles as we move from lower- to higher-level cognition . (Schoner & Spencer 2015)

Furthermore, in Clare (in press) grounds the cognitive dynamics of "Dynamic Field theory" to the actor via the notion of "attention-field" as follows:

> The Group outlines different types of "attention-fields" – spatial attention-fields, scene attention-fields, feature attention-fields, transformation attention-fields, contrast fields retinal fields within which attentional foregrounding, hills and peaks of activation, and sequential transitions occur. Although these are short-term attention-fields, they can be related to the constructed attention-field of the actor, a long-term, artificially sustained field with a complex contextual function ... Other relevant aspects of DFT include descriptions of working memory fields as feature, spatial, or scene ... In a chapter on Integrating perception-action with cognition (pp. 197–226), Schneegans, Spencer, and Schoner address the attention-field and working memory patterns of individuals in relation to objects in the real world – it would be extremely useful to extend this to imagined objects and the conceptual world within which actors function and construct the lives of their parts over time.

4. On autopoiesis and allopoiesis

4.1. Autopoiesis or self-creation

Maturana and Varela's original definition of autopoiesis is found in Maturana & Varela (1973):

> An autopoietic machine is a machine organized (defined as a unity) as a network of processes of production (transformation and destruction) of components which: (i) through their interactions and transformations continuously regenerate and realize the network of processes (relations) that produced them; and (ii) constitute it (the machine) as a concrete unity in space in which they (the components) exist by specifying the topological domain of its realization as such a network. (p. 78)

Thus, the boundary of an autopoietic system is determined circularly by the production of its constituent elements; in this way the organisation of, say, a cell is both "circular" and autopoietic because the components that specify the cell are the same components that the organisation of the cell secures and maintains. It is this circularity that maintains the cell as a *living* entity. It is in this sense that an autopoietic system can be considered as a special type of *homeostatic system*, where the variable to be maintained and controlled is the *organisation and behaviour* of the system. For Francisco Varela, autopoiesis is both necessary and sufficient to characterise the organisation of *living, autonomous* systems.

In addition to maintaining the conditions for its own continued existence, an autopoietic system may, in addition, generate *allopoietic system(s)* as output(s).

4.2. Allopoiesis

In contrast to autopoiesis, the operation of an allopoietic system is given in terms of the concatenation of processes. Such processes are not the processes that specify the components of the system itself, as a unity; instead the components are produced by other processes that are independent of the organisation of the system. Because the components that make up an allopoietic system's existence are contingent upon other systems, an allopoietic system is never "fully autonomous". Some examples of allopoietic systems are: cars, trains, robots, etc.

Furthermore, because an allopoietic system is always contingent on the output of other systems for it existence, its teleology and meaning will always reside in the observers world, never in its own – the systems – world.

4.3. On the autopoietic status of systems

To determine whether a system is or is not autopoietic in its organisation, Varela, Maturana, and Uribe (1974) have developed six key points or criteria that should be applied to the system; Koskinen (2010) restates these criteria as follows:

(1) Determine, through interactions, if the unity has identifiable boundaries. If the boundaries can be determined, proceed to 2. If not, the entity is indescribable and we can say nothing.
(2) Determine if there are constitutive elements of the unity, that is, components of the unity. If these components can be described, proceed to 3. If not, the unity is an unanalysable whole and therefore not an autopoietic system.
(3) Determine if the unity is a mechanistic system, that is, if the component properties are capable of satisfying certain relations that determine the unity, the interactions, and transformations of these components. If this is the case, proceed to 4. If not, the unity is not an autopoietic system.
(4) Determine if the components that constitute the boundaries of the unity constitute these boundaries through preferential neighbourhood relations and interactions between themselves, as determined by their properties in the space of their interactions. If this is not the case, you do not have an autopoietic unity because you are determining its boundaries, not the unity itself. If 4 is the case, however, proceed to 5.

(5) Determine if the components of the boundaries of the unity are produced by the interactions of the components of the unity, either by transformation of previously produced components, or by transformations and/ or coupling of non-component elements that enter the unity through its boundaries. If not, you do not have an autopoietic unity; if yes, proceed to 6.

(6) If all the other components of the unity are also produced by the interactions of its components as in 5, and if those which are not produced by the interactions of other components participate as necessary permanent constitutive components in the production of other components, you have an autopoietic unity *in the space in which its components exist*. If this is not the case and there are components in the unity not produced by components of the unity as in 5, or if there are components of the unity which do not participate in the production of other components, you do not have an autopoietic unity.

Thus, the successful application of the above six-point taxonomy is sufficient to determine if a system is autopoietically organised (or not).

5. Luhmann: autopoeisis and social systems

In formulating his *law of requisite variety*, Ashby (1956) observed that to survive in a complex environment while maintaining internal stability and structure, a system must be able to generate an appropriate gamut of responses to an ever-changing environment. In contrast, General Systems Theory, as formulated by Bertalanffy (1968), assumes an *open systems model*,[6] viewing complex systems in terms of the difference between "the system and its environment" ; contra a *closed system model* [7] and mereological distinctions between, say, the physical instantiation of "whole and parts".

Influenced by General Systems Theory, the core element of Niklas Luhmann's "system theoretic" view of social systems is communication: social systems *are* systems of communication and society *is* the most encompassing social system. In Luhmann's (1995b) view a social system is defined by the boundary between itself and its environment, which is considered an infinitely complex ("chaotic") exterior. Thus, relative to the exterior, the interior of the social system is a space of reduced complexity: communication within a social system operates by selecting only a limited element of all the information available outside the system. In this way Luhmann's concept of communication inherently entails a "reduction of complexity", whereby the criteria according to which information is selected and processed is *meaning*. Thus social systems are *operationally closed* because, while they use and rely on resources from their environment, those resources do not become an integral part of the systems' operation.

Thus for Luhmann, social systems operate by processing meaning and furthermore, each system has a distinctive identity; a unity, that is constantly reproduced in its communication and depends on what is considered meaningful (and what is not) for that system. If the system fails to maintain this identity, it dies, it ceases to exist and it dissolves back into the wider environmental ether whence it came.

Luhmann conceived this process of continuous reproduction from elements previously filtered from an over-complex environment as *autopoiesis*.[8]

5.1. Social cognition and autopoietic enactivism

Furthermore, by demonstrating how consciousness and subjective experience are related to the brain and body of an organism in *enactivist theory*, Thompson (2007) binds the notion of autopoiesis to consciousness – not just cognition.

> ... our environment is one which we selectively create through our capacities to interact with the world. Organisms do not passively receive information from their environments, which they then translate into internal representations. Natural cognitive systems ... participate in the generation of meaning ... by engaging in transformational, and not merely informational, interactions; they enact a world.

In this light, and following De Jaegher & Di Paolo (2007) have extended the enactive concept of "sense-making " (Thompson, 2007) into the cultural domain, whereby De Jaegher and Di Paolo argue that *the interaction process itself* can take on a form of autonomy (operationally [autopoietically] defined). This allows us to consider *autopoiesis in creativity* as the generation of meaning and its transformation through individuals interacting [within a dance-field].

6. "Creativity" as an autopoietic process

6.1. Historical

The resonance of art with autpoiesis has been explored by several thinkers, most notably Luhmann who in his theory of social systems (Luhmann, 1996) famously put forward a "theory of art" as *a particular system of communication*, i.e. ... *the function of art can be traced to problems of meaningful communication* (Luhmann, 1995a). For Luhmann, the domain of art is to be viewed as an operationally closed and self-referential communicative system, an autopoietic system; radically suggesting that it is "... from the autopoiesis of art which works of art will be created". This led Rampley, in his review (Rampley, 2009), to suggest that the ' ... key question Luhmann addresses [in his conception of art and autopoiesis]is how art differentiates itself from other systems '.

A traditional, representation-heavy, view of the artist as an open-system, fundamentally posits the artist's activities as contingent on external influences; the artist responds creatively to demands from a pre-given, objective environment by building and creatively processing appropriate internal representations. In this view, through his art, the artist builds representations of a pre-given reality – universal, objective, and transferable – and it is his role, as artist, to transform these representations in novel, interesting and creative ways.

The contrary, autopoietic perspective reflects that creativity is autonomous and operationally closed.[9] In addition, autopoietic creative systems stand "structurally coupled" with their medium; fundamentally embedded in a dynamic of changes, exercised via appropriate sense-action coupling. This continuous dynamic can be considered a rudimentary form of *creative knowledge*.

Emerging from a *General System Theory* perspective, the exploration of autopoiesis in the context of "creativity studies" was first outlined by Gornev (1997) who first set out to construct a theory of human creativity on the foundation of autopoietic systems theory (AST), whereby:

> creativity is seen as an activity recurrently reproduced by couplings of specific states of moderate emotional arousal with transitional environments, i.e. soft social structures in which the

world is permitted to be both subjective and objective; the archetype of these creative couplings can be found in the earliest perfect environment formed by the symbiotic infant/mother relationship.

In contrast Iba (2010) defined "Creative Systems Theory" in order to view *creative processes* [10] in an alternative way, . . . *focusing the process itself without the reference to psychic or social aspects*. In his work Iba postulated *creative processes* to be "autopoietic systems whose elements are *discoveries* emerged by a synthesis of three selections: *idea, association, and consequence*".

However, by merely defining that "creativity is an autopoietic system whose element is *discovery*", Iba's work, like Gornev's first tentative explorations 13 years earlier, remains floating very much at a conceptual level; it offers little insight into how "creative process" at the personal, "psychic", *artistic* level could ever actually be cached out; indeed, as he stated in the paper (Iba, 2010), this was never his project.

6.2. *Our view*

Conversely, and in an analogous manner to Luhmann's conception of *information processing*, we view *creativity* as entailing a reduction in complexity of meaning in the environment; with the system operationally closed because, while its creativity uses and relies upon resources from its environment, these resources do not become part of the underlying systems' operation.

Viewed under this conception, a creative system (a) processes *meaning* and (b) maintains a distinctive identity; a unity that is repeatedly reproduced in its operation, contingent upon what is considered meaningful (or not) for the system. If the environmental conditions are such that, over time, the creative system can no longer maintain this identity, then its investigations will simply *dissolve away* to void.

In this way creativity is a *constructive process*; it inherently reflects an *individually constructed artistic reality*. Furthermore, because autopoietic creativity emerges from the observation of *distinctions* and not of *things*, its operation is fundamentally contingent on its own history, and in this way is ever-sensitive to its own historical context.

In summary, and in contrast to the classical view of creative processes building (reflecting on and transforming) representations of a pre-given, out-there, world, an autopoietic view of creativity is based on the simultaneous knowledge processes of *sensing* and *memory*. In this context memory[11] entails that:

- the unity has access to its existing knowledge;
- previous, accumulated, knowledge modulates the unity's ongoing structures and operations;
- the unity's cognitive structures and operation affect its acquisition of new data from the environment and its creation of new internal knowledge structures.

Furthermore, we observe that by conceptualising creative processes within an autopoietic framework, we must conclude that *creativity* is never a directly transferable skill or knowledge.[12]

7. Autopoiesis, creativity and dance

In our work we examine a dancer, typically working with a rehearsal director, a choreographer, who guides the dancer's movements. We consider the *space* defined by the dancer's state-of-mind, the dancer's movements and teacher's movements as the *dance-field*.[13] The continual *creative processes* of attention and reconstitution (movement) mechanisms that act in this field are detailed in the accompanying paper (in the context of "the Autopoietic Artist" – a "weakly creative" computational drawing system) (al-Rifaie et al., in press).

We see in Figure 2 Jo, one of the rehearsal Directors of this production of *Kontakthof*, working with one of the students, and draw the reader's attention to three observations from the scene:

(1) From her expression, it is apparent that the dancer is both deeply engaged and acutely feeling the creative process.
(2) There appears to be a diminution of the dancer's subjective self, as her concentration and bodily-control bring-forth a deeply engaged coupling between her actions, the choreographer's intent and her environment.
(3) The precariousness and temporal boundedness of the creative act. Eventually in the rehearsal, we see the dancer's coupling dissipate as she returns to her normal, subjective, self-critical state: a 'being in time'.

8. The autopoietic dancer as a "strongly" creative system

We view the creative, guided-improvisations of the "autopoietic" dancer as being primarily directed by two functionally distinct processes: (i) a process of attention whereby the dancers "cognitive resources" are drawn to (potentially multiple) elements of meaning-distinction in the dance-field that are *in some sense* important to the dancer (in al-Rifaie et al., in press we suggest this could be computationally realised by stochastic diffusion processes (Bishop, 1989); see the appendix and (ii) a process of *interpretation* whereby a movement is (re) interpreted by the dancer in her performance (a process which in al-Rifaie et al., in press we suggest could be computationally realised by a "particle swarm"; see the

Figure 2. Image of young dancer in *Kontakthof* as she listens to feedback from Jo, one the rehearsal Directors ("Dancing Dreams", (c) Real Fiction 2010).

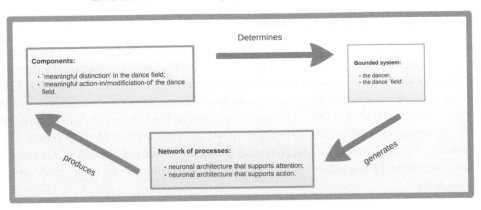

Figure 3. Autopoiesis in creativity and dance.

appendix for Algorithm A1). Elements of the dance-field that are most meaningful/impor-tant to the dancer (at this particular instant in time) will attract the most cognitive resources, resulting in these elements to be attended to next by the (re)interpretation processes controlling the dancer's movement(s).

NB. It is a natural consequence of considering the dancer's control of her creative move-ments as an autopoietic process defined in this way, that a skilled dancer/performer will find some aspects of movement relatively simple (less interesting/meaningful) and hence not deploy so much cognitive resources to their (re)interpretation as a dancer relatively new to the movement; in this way the skilled dancer is thus free to redeploy resources in more meaningful areas of performance, perhaps focussing on perfecting the technicalities of a particularly difficult movement, or perhaps focussing on synthesising her movements *as a whole*, etc.

In this manner the "autopoietic" dancer is thus continually engaged in a process of sens-ing her environment (the dance-field) and reconstituting it (by iteratively first choosing a gesture of meaning and (re)interpreting it); hence Varela et al.'s criteria (Varela et al., 1974) for an autopoietic entity are appropriately instantiated in the cognitive processes of the "autopoietic" dancer acting *in the space in which her creative unity exists*.

Over time, with her "interest" drawn to areas rich in meaning (peculiar to her), the autopoietic dancer, so construed, iteratively reinterprets meaningful-distinctions (gestures) in her current dance-field, so offering a very personal reinterpretation of the structure of the work. Over time though, inevitably less of the dance-field will continue to offer up meaningful-distinctions, at which point the dancer's attention becomes gradually less focussed as her creative process stultify and eventually cease; reifying the movements' "death" and returning the dancer to silence. Thus, following Luhmann's conception of *infor-mation processing*, we view the working autopoietic dancer as inevitably entailing a reduc-tion in complexity, ravenously consuming "meaning-distinctions" within her environment (the dance-field) until none remain and movement ends . . .

In this light (see Figure 3) the autopoietic model, we suggest offers a new account of creativity in terms of an operationally closed, casual circularity between three core groups of elements:

(a) *The creative-actor as a bounded system consisting of*:

- the actor [dancer];
- an "attention-field" [dance-field] comprised of a multitude of potential "meaningful-distinctions".

... which generates ...

(b) *A network of processes*:
- neural processes that support attention;
- neural processes that support action.

... which produces ...

(c) *Components*:
- "meaningful distinctions" in the attention-field [dance-field];
- "meaningful actions" in (and hence modification of) the attention-field [dance-field].

... which [cyclically] update and together co-determine the bounded system ...

And we suggest that it is this – the dancer and her environment as a bounded system, an autopoietic unity – that precariously brings forth the phenomenology of her movement, alongside its inevitable dissipation ...

9. Conclusion

In conclusion, in the context of al-Rifaie and Bishop's "weak" and "strong" taxonomy of [computational] creativity (al-Rifaie & Bishop, 2015), we suggest autopoiesis offers a new conception of "strong" creativity in movement and dance. This new autopoietic, enactive conception offers insights into (a) the phenomenality of the creative process – why it *feels like* something to create; (b) the *altered state of the creative process* – in this context Merleau-Ponty's "entre-deux" conceptualises the state as being neither fully objective of subjective and (c) the *time-bounded period of creativity* as the autopoietic creative processes inevitably decays back to void. Furthermore, and in contrast to the computational autopoietic artist (al-Rifaie et al., in press), because the dancer's biologically "strongly embodied" (Ziemke, 2001) cognitive processes select areas of *meaning distinction* that are, in her current context, paradigmatically meaningful *to her*, the autopoietic dancer – richly embodied in her environment, the dance-field – constitutes a fully autonomous *strongly creative* system.

Notes

1. Although, of course, interpretation can be an *emergent property* of such action.
2. This paper forms the left-hand side of a diptych in which, herein, we offer autopoiesis as a new light under which to view creative processes in richly embodied movement and dance; a *philosophical exegesis* of the core generic concepts relating autopoiesis and creativity first discussed at AISB2016, Sheffield UK; cf. Bishop & al-Rifaie, *Autopoiesis, creativity and Dance* (Bishop and al-Rifaie in press). The original conceptual driver - relating swarm intelligence and autopoiesis - first emerged in work by al-Rifaie and Bishop [on swarmic sketching] and subsequent discussions on

computational art with Leymarie and Latham. Conversely, forming the right hand side of the diptych (and working alongside Frederic Leymarie and William Latham) we instantiate the autopoietic metaphor of creativity via a specific computational mechanism and successfully deploy this to improvise new computational sketches al-Rifaie, Leymarie, Latham, and Bishop (in press).

3. For Whitehead, all real objects may be better understood as a constructed series of events and processes. It is this core idea that Whitehead explains the seminal "Process and Reality" (Whitehead 1929), concluding that it is process, rather than substance, that should be taken as the most fundamental metaphysical constituent of the world,

> That "all things flow" is the first vague generalisation which the unsystematised, barely analysed, intuition of men has produced. Without doubt, if we are to go back to that ultimate, integral experience, unwarped by the sophistications of theory, that experience whose elucidation is the final aim of philosophy, the flux of things is one ultimate generalisation around which we must weave our philosophical system. (Whitehead 1929, p. 317)

4. . . . in much the same way as Koskinen identifies that all business organisations eventually wither, dissolve away and ultimately die

> . . . decisions have to be imagined as events. In the very moment of their coming into being, they already fade away. Therefore, only little can be changed in business organisations. As decisions disappear with their appearance, they cannot be altered, but only give cause for the production of new decisions, which are subject to the same mechanism. And this is the reason why business organisations step by step wither and die. (K.U. Koskinen, "Why do Business Organizations die? Social Autopoietic Perspective").

5. As Clare (in press) observes

> Jacob von Uexkull labelled perception of the world, experienced by and through the capacity of species-specific bodies, the umwelt: literally surround-world. That is to say it is inherently embodied because it is biologically limited by the sensory apparatus of the physical body.

Stanislavsky, developing a system of practice for the actor, that was in opposition to purely representational modes of melodrama, offered one of the first modes of training that

> . . . implicitly addresses this very subject, teaching the student to contextualise their individual umwelt within a wider framework of the human umwelt: the spatial adpositional umwelt. This both frames the acting process and opens the students awareness to what is humanly possible. (Clare, in press)

6. An open system exchanges material, energy, people, capital, information, etc. with its environment.

7. A closed system does not allow transfers in out of the system.

8. NB. Both Varela and Maturana have forcefully argued against this appropriation of the term autopoiesis; in Maturana and Varela's conception, people cannot be proper elements of a social system's renewal because (a) in describing social systems as operationally closed networks of communications, Luhmann ignores the fact that communications presuppose *human* communicators (Maturana & Poerkson, 2004) and (b) people are not *(re)produced* as an integral and core part of a social system's renewal processes (Maula, 2006).

9. It is operationally close in the sense that there are sufficient processes within it to maintain the unity of creation and that, while they use (and rely upon) resources from their environment, those resources do not themselves become an integral core element of the creative systems' operation.

10. Iba defines that a creative process consists of "a sequence of discoveries, which include problem finding, problem solving, observation, hypothesis formation, method selection, practice, and interpretation". (Iba, 2010)

11. A *self-referential* process which facilitates access to, and learning from, previous experiences and knowledge (Koskinen 2010).

12. Cf. Koskinen on "autopoietic knowledge systems in project-based companies" (Koskinen 2010)

13. Mathematically imagined represented as a complex manifold.

Disclosure statement

No potential conflict of interest was reported by the authors.

References

al-Rifaie, M. M., & Bishop, J. M. (2013). Stochastic diffusion search review. *Journal of Behavioural Robotics, 4*(3), 155–173.

al-Rifaie, M. M., & Bishop, J. M. (2015). Weak and strong computational creativity. In T. R. Besold, M. Schorlemmer, & A. Smaill (Eds.), *Computational creativity research. Towards creative machines* (pp. 37–51). Springer.

al-Rifaie, M. M., Leymarie, F., Latham, W., & Bishop, J. M. (in press). Swarmic autopoiesis and computational creativity. *Connection Science*. doi:10.1080/09540091.2016.1274960

Ashby, W. R. (1956). *An introduction to cybernetics*. London: Chapman and Hall.

Bertalanffy, L. von. (1968). *General system theory: Foundations, development, applications*. New York, NY: George Braziller. revised edition 1976: ISBN 0-8076-0453-4.

Bishop, J. M. (1989). Stochastic searching networks. *Proceedings of the first IEEE international conference on artificial neural networks* (pp. 329–331) (October 16–18), London, UK.

Bishop, J. M., & al-Rifaie, M. M. (2016). Autopoiesis, creativity and dance. *Proceedings of the AISB 2016: 3rd symposium on embodied cognition, acting and performance*, Sheffield, UK.

Clare, Y. (in press). Stanislavskys system as an enactive guide to embodied cognition: A framework for comparisons. *Proceedings of the AISB 2016: 3rd symposium on embodied cognition, acting and performance*, Sheffield, UK. *Connection Science*.

De Jaegher, H., & Di Paolo, E. (2007). Participatory sense-making: An enactive approach to social cognition. *Phenomenology and the Cognitive Sciences, 6*(4), 485–507.

Gornev, G. P. (1997). The creativity question in the perspective of autopoietic systems theory. *Kybernetes, 26*(6/7), 738–750.

Iba, T. (2010). An autopoietic systems theory for creativity. *Proceedings of the COINs2009: Collaborative innovation networks conference published in, procedia social and behavioral sciences*, Vol. 2 (pp. 6610–6625).

Koskinen, K. U. (2010). *Autopoietic knowledge systems in project-based companies*. Palgrave Macmillan.

Luhmann, N. (1995a). *Social systems*. Stanford, CA: Stanford University Press.

Luhmann, N. (1995b). *Gesellschaftsstruktur und Semantik 4: Studien zur Wissenssoziologie der modernen Gesellschaft (Structure of Society and Semantic 4: Studies on Knowledge-Sociology of Modern Society)*. Frankfurt am Main: Suhrkamp.

Luhmann, N. (1996). *Die Kunst der Gesellschaft*. Frankfurt a. M: Suhrkamp.

Maturana, H., & Varela, F. (1973). De Mquinas y Seres Vivos: Una teor'a de la organizac'on biol-gica. Santiago de Chile: Editorial Universitaria. [Reprinted in English in Maturana, H., & Varela, F. (1980). *Autopoiesis and cognition: The realization of the living*. Boston, MA: D.Reidel.].

Maturana, H., & Poerkson, B. (2004). *From being to doing: The origins of the biology of cognition*. Carl Auer International (pp. 105–108). ISBN: 3896704486.

Maula, M. (2006). *Organizations as learning systems: Living composition as an enabling infrastructure (advanced series in management)*. Elsevier.

Moglich, M., Maschwitz, U., & Holldobler, B. (1974). Tandem calling: A new kind of signal in ant communication. *Science, 186*(4168), 1046–1047.

Rampley, M. (2009). Art as a social system: The sociological Aesthetics of Niklas Luhmann. *Telos, 148*, 111–140.

Schoner, G., & Spencer, J. and the DFT Research Group. (2015). *Dynamic thinking: A primer on dynamic field theory*. Oxford: Oxford University Press.

Shi, Y., & Eberhart, R. C. (1998). A modified particle swarm optimizer. *Proceedings of the IEEE International Conference on Evolutionary Computation* (pp. 69–73). Piscataway, NJ: IEEE Press.

Thompson, E. (2007). *Mind in life*. MA: Harvard University Press, Cambridge.

Varela, F. J., Maturana, H. R., & Uribe, R. (1974). Autopoiesis: The organization of living systems, its characterization and a model. *Biosystems, 5*(4), 187–96.

Varela, F. J., Thompson, E., & Rosch, E. (1991). *The embodied mind: Cognitive science and human experience*. The MIT Press.

Wallas, G. (1926), *Art of Thought* (reprinted by Solis Press 2014).

Whitehead, A. N. (1929). *Process and reality*. New York, NY: Macmillan.

Ziemke, T. (2001), *Disentangling notions of embodiment*. Workshop on Developmental Embodied Cognition, Edinburgh, UK, July 2001.

Appendix. Stochastic diffusion search

This section introduces Stochastic Diffusion Search (Bishop 1989) – a swarm intelligence algorithm – whose performance is based on simple interaction of agents. This algorithm is inspired by one species of ants, *Leptothorax acervorum*, where a "tandem calling" mechanism (one-to-one communication) is used, the forager ant that finds the food location recruits a single ant upon its return to the nest; therefore the location of the food is physically publicised Moglich, Maschwitz, and Holldobler (1974).

SDS is an efficient Swarm Intelligence global-search meta-heuristic (al-Rifaie & Bishop 2013), which we deploy herein to search for "meaningful distinctions" in the dance-field. The principles of can be most easily illustrated via analogy. Consider, "The Bar Game":

> A group of delegates attend a conference on computing and movement in Thessaloniki and want to spend their evenings at the best bar in town; Thessaloniki, for those who are new to its charms, has a huge number of great bars and each delegate will have their own taste defining what constitutes a good bar and a good night out.
>
> Initially, each delegate adopts a random hypothesis of the best bar in town and visits that bar that night.
>
> At the end of the evening each delegate merely needs to decide if they had a good evening or not (a stochastic decision informed on a subjective assessment of the bar and its clientele). That is, unless the bar is deemed 'perfect' by the delegate, there is a non-zero probability that, over time, even a good bar may result in a bad evening; nonetheless, across the population – ceteris paribus – delegates are likely to keep returning to a 'good' bar . . .
>
> The next morning each delegate who didn't like the bar they visited, asks a randomly selected co-delegate, if they had a good time the previous evening; if they did they simply adopt their fellow delegate's hypothesis, otherwise they simply reselect a new "best-bar" hypothesis at random.
>
> It can be shown that over a relatively short period of time a stochastic diffusion process (such as this) will converge, and a stable population of delegates will assemble on the best bar in town . . . .

More formally, the algorithm commences a search or optimisation by initialising its population and then iterating through two phases (see Algorithm1)

Algorithm 1 Algorithm

```
01: Initialise agents
02: While (stopping condition is not met)
04:     For each agent
03:         Test hypothesis and determine activity
05:     For each agent
06:         Diffuse hypothesis
07: End While
```

In the *test phase* of each iteration, checks whether the agent hypothesis is successful or not by performing a hypothesis evaluation which returns a boolean value. In the *diffusion phase*, contingent on the precise recruitment strategy employed, successful hypotheses diffuse across the population and in this way information on potentially good solutions spreads throughout the entire population of agents.

A. Particle Swarm Optimisation

A PSO is a swarm intelligence optimisation process, whose broad principles of operation we can illustrate with the following simple analogy:

Imagine that one dips a finger in a jar of honey and uses that honeyed-finger to trace a line in the air in the presence of a swarm of bees. Fairly soon the bees will begin to buzz around the honeyed finger tip. By using this swarm we can generate a new series of points (defining a new line) simply by noting the centroid of this swarm at successive instants in time.

More formally, a swarm in Particle Swarm Optimisation (PSO) algorithm comprises of a number of particles and each particle represents a point in a multi-dimensional problem space. Particles in the swarm explore the problem space searching for the optimal position, which is defined by a fitness function.

Each particle has a position x, a velocity v, and a memory, p, containing the best position found so far during the course of the optimisation, and this is called the personal best (pbest). p can also be thought of as a particle "informer". Particles participate in a social information sharing network. Each particle is informed by its neighbours within this network, and in particular, the best position so far found in the neighbourhood, is termed the neighbourhood best. The position of each particle is dependent on the particle's own experience and those of its neighbours.

The standard PSO algorithm defines the position of each particle by adding a velocity to the current position. Here is the equation for updating the velocity of each particle:

$$v_{id}^{t} = w v_{id}^{t-1} + c_1 r_1 (p_{id} - x_{id}^{t-1}) + c_2 r_2 (g_{id} - x_{id}^{t-1}), \qquad (A1)$$

$$x_{id}^{t} = v_{id}^{t} + x_{id}^{t-1}, \qquad (A2)$$

where w is the inertia weight whose optimal value is problem dependent (Shi & Eberhart 1998) ; $\vec{v}_{id}^{t-1}$ is the velocity component of particle i in dimension d at time step $t-1$; $c_{1,2}$ are the learning factors (also referred to as acceleration constants) for personal best and neighbourhood best, respectively (they are constant); $r_{1,2}$ are random numbers adding stochasticity to the algorithm and they are drawn from a uniform distribution on the unit interval $U(0,1)$; p_{id} is the personal best position of particle x_i in dimension d; and g_{id} is the neighbourhood best. Therefore, PSO optimisation is based on particles' individual experience and their social interaction with other particles. After position and velocity updates, the positions of the particles are evaluated and the memories p are updated, if a better position has been found.

COMMENTARY

Embodiment: a cross-disciplinary provocation

Deirdre McLaughlin

Thirty years ago this provocation would not have been written. Embodiment has grown rapidly throughout the course of the past three decades into a relevant and challenging concept intersecting a range of disciplines and research programmes responding to its development. This provocation explores select theories of embodiment from the embodied cognition research programme as well as some practical processes and conceptual applications of embodiment from the field of actor training and actor-based performance training. I am largely responding to the work presented at the Embodied Cognition, Acting and Performance Symposium for which this Special Edition of Connection Science is an outcome. The articulations of the term embodiment currently inform two separate disciplinary understandings of this concept. Here, I highlight a move towards cross-disciplinary approaches to the concept of embodiment and offer an integrative new articulation of the term, bridging received divided between these two distinct and ever developing fields. This provocation argues that embodiment offers a valuable and challenging dimension to our emerging interdisciplinary discourse and that embodied processes are central to the ongoing integration of these two disciplines. This focus on our ongoing interdisciplinary strategies subsequently invites the proposition that embodiment, as an issue of central importance to both disciplinary spheres, may indeed be the key to any future transdisciplinary developments in research and practice occurring between the distinct fields of embodied cognition and performance practice.

Defining embodiment

The fact that embodiment has emerged as a primary issue for consideration in both cognitive science and actor training (and actor-based performance training) as just two examples of a wider range of disciplines and research programmes grappling with this concept reflects a concrete change in thinking about the nature of the mind and cognitive processing which extends beyond individual disciplinary projects. In many ways, the concept of embodiment has served as a pivotal catalyst or fulcrum between various disciplines within the sciences, arts, and humanities, from early work on embodied cognition and metaphors (Lakoff & Johnson, 1980), enactive perspectives of cognition

(Varela, Thompson, & Rosch, 1991), and more contemporary approaches to philosophy of mind (Shapiro, 2014). This special edition includes a contribution by our esteemed collaborator Shaun Gallagher whose seminal *How the Body Shapes the Mind* (2005) has served as a model of interdisciplinary scholarship, exploring embodiment across a variety of disciplines, including neuroscience, behavioural psychology, artificial intelligence and robotics, and phenomenology and philosophy of mind, arguing for the development of a common vocabulary as well as a conceptual framework from which we might determine the extent to which our consciousness and cognitive processes are shaped and structured by our embodiment. This is a position shared by this provocation whose specific approach is developed at the intersection of the embodied cognition research programme and actor training.

In his contribution to *The Cambridge handbook of cognitive science* (Clark, 2012), Clark, a key player in the development of embodiment in the cognitive sciences (1997, 2010, 2016), addresses some of the philosophical issues which underpin the fast emergence of embodiment as a primary concept under consideration within the development of the embodied cognition research programme that additionally function across a variety disciplinary fields.

> Flesh and world are surely flavors of the moment. Talk of mind as intimately embodied and profoundly environmentally embedded shimmers at the cusp of the cognitive scientific zeitgeist. But beneath the glamour and glitz lies a still-murky vision. For this view of mind can seem by turns radical and trivial, interestingly true and outrageously false, scientifically important and a mere distraction, philosophically challenging and simply confused … [and yet we must] attempt to locate some footholds in this new and at times treacherous landscape. It is comforting to begin with a seeming truth. Human minds, it can hardly be doubted, are at the very least in deep and critically important contact with human bodies and with the wider world. Human sensing, learning, thought, and feeling are all structured and informed by our body-based interactions with the world around us. (Clark, 2012, p. 275)

This allure of the embodiment as a concept extends beyond the cognitive sciences, and while its theoretical underpinnings within the arts may have a similarly "murky" vision in terms of their linguistic application, attempts to identify clear footholds within many of our actor training systems remain. Furthermore, while the identification of enactive and environmentally embedded approaches to cognition may on the surface appear to be limited to a small score of performance theorists, including the likes of Blair (2007), Kemp (2012), Lutterbie (2011), McConachie (2008, 2013), and McConachie and Hart (2006), the conviction that cognition "is not the representation of a pre-given world by a pre-given mind but is rather the enactment of a world and a mind on the basis of a history of the variety of actions that a being in the world performs" (Varela et al., 1992, p. 9) is exhibited within a wide range of actor training systems and techniques which privilege "the process of experiencing" (Stanislavski, 2008, p. 23) and "organic acting" (Gillett, 2014) with its focus on action and the recreation of human experience within a set of given circumstances (i.e. "a pregiven world") over representational acting and its dependence of pretending, imitation, and creating physical and emotional states.

As conceptual applications of embodiment remain the focus of this provocation, it is important to note that some commentators, including contributors to this special edition Shaun Gallagher and J. Mark Bishop, view Andy Clark's "extended mind" position as effectively subscribing to an etiolated notion of embodiment – a so-called weak embodiment. As a contrast to weak embodiment, Sharkey and Ziemke's (2000) identify "strong embodiment" as the position that not only does the body shape cognition, but the matter of the body is constitutive of cognitive processes. This argument is shared by Nasuto and Bishop (2011) who forcefully make the case that the actual substance of embodiment matter greatly to the grounding of our cognition. Conversely, weak embodiment is "the view that concepts are not represented only by sensory/motor processes, but are also represented at an abstract or modality-independent level" (Mahon, 2014, p. 1), a position which may be viewed effectively as computationalism revisited though the back-door. In his contribution to this special edition, Shaun Gallagher states that "Clark's (2008) conception of the extended mind builds on a functionalist view that downplays the role of the biological body – cognition could be instantiated in a robotic body, for example" (Gallagher, 2017). However, Clark's inclusion in this dialogue is to provide a specific insight into his framing interdisciplinary conceptualisations of embodiment rather than to argue directly or indirectly for the application of his view of extended cognition.

Clark continues his inciting call to further the landscape of embodiment studies by drawing on Esther Thelan's popular framing of the embodied perspective in which she states that "to say cognition is embodied means that it arises from bodily interactions within the world" (2000, p. 4). Clark posits that while it is unlikely that many would disagree with Thelan's statement given current trends in discourses surrounding embodiment, it is essential that we further interrogate this frequently cited position in order to gain a more comprehensive view of some of the "radical" arguments which underlie it. To provide further context for consideration, Thelan goes on to state that:

> From this point of view, cognition depends on the kinds of experiences that come from having a body with particular perceptual and motor capacities that are inseparably linked and that together form the matrix within which memory, emotion, language, and all other aspects of life are *meshed*. The contemporary motion of embodied cognition stands in contrast to the prevailing cognitivist stance which sees the mind as a device to manipulate symbols and is thus concerned with the formal rules and processes by which symbols appropriately represent the word. (2000, my italics)

The key point which Clark aims to highlight here is not that cognition is body dependent or informed by the experience of our individual perceptual and motor capacities, but rather the implications of the word "meshing" as signalling an "intermingling of cognitive activity" (Clark, 2012, p. 276). It is this intermingling, or meshing, of mind, body, and world that is perhaps the most radical offering of the embodied cognition research programme, the argument for cognitive processes to be framed within an "embodied dynamism" which focuses on agents as self-organising dynamic systems and "maintains in addition that cognitive processes emerge from the nonlinear and circular causality of continuous sensorimotor interactions involving brain, body, and environment" (Thompson, 2007, p. 10–11). The emergence of embodied dynamism and the development of an enactive approach marked significant shifts in the development of cognitive science and our shared conception of embodiment which would later receive popular applications within research in performance practice and actor training – and yet, when given a more detailed look, it is these dynamic developments within the embodied cognition research programme which have been central to the practical *doing* of acting and actor training, as one specific example of performance practice, for over 100 years.

Embodied cognition and actor training: a cross-disciplinary approach to embodiment

In contemporary actor training discourse, it is in currently quite fashionable to examine embodiment and embodied phenomena as they relate to the actor's process. To be fair, it is in fashion within many performance disciplines, but to focus my point, I have chosen to concentrate here on acting and western actor training techniques and systems as they provide a productive point of departure for exploring the nature of embodiment as a system for understanding human experience and cognition. Rick Kemp, performance maker, scholar, and contributor to this special edition, argues for the ongoing development of a cross-disciplinary dialogue between cognitive science and performance practice in his 2012 text *Embodied Acting*.

> The scientific investigation of the mind and brain offers theatre people better ways of understanding the psychophysical processes involved in performance. Cognitive science also offers us tools with which to describe the distinctions between different approaches as well as to recognize fundamental similarities among them ... Furthermore, the understanding that cognitive science offers us is one that acknowledges the central role of the body, and helps us to better understand the relationships between thought and expression, a subject that is hazily expressed in most theories of acting. (Kemp, 2012 p. 15)

Kemp acknowledges that while the recreation of human experience is central to many technical systems of acting, making them fertile ground for theoretical applications of cognitive science and more specifically, embodied cognition to this performance practice, how these are expressed within articulated theories of acting remains at best hazy. This is in part because most of the writing which exists on the acting process is split between two distinct camps: practical guides to acting technique and theoretical views on acting and performance employing scientific, philosophical, cultural, political, and historical perspectives. Indeed, it is in this division of practice and theory whereby conceptions of embodiment within actor training have had the tendency to become confused as the nature of their embodied processes and their "meshing" becomes challenging to frame without an engagement across these fields of research and practice.

> The concept of the embodied mind is one that fundamentally alters the mind/body split on which twentieth-century approaches to actor training are based ... Many practitioners have been working psychophysically – but the concepts and terms that they use to describe this work have been bound by the "internal/external" dichotomy. Creating a cognitive vocabulary for theatrical activities would support a language of theatre that applies to a variety of styles because it is based on foundational cognitive activities. (17–18)

At first glance, this idea is far from new and the argument for an embodied mind holds strong resonances for existing performance and actor training practices. Historically, virtually all post-Stanislavski systems of actor training identify directly or indirectly the dynamic relationship between the actor's mind, body, and world using terms such as embodiment, psychophysical, and integrated processes. However, these systems have been largely bound by training languages which have not developed with the same sense of immediacy as many of the theoretical fields from upon which they draw. Thus, their concepts and language do not always reflect the advancement of knowledge which can be located within their practice. This may be one reason why some performance researchers have received criticism for using cognitive science to "justify" their practice, when in fact they may fallen into this hierarchical exchange whereby cognitive science is used as a means of validating thinking around and through performance due to the limits of the language surrounding their practice. The limits of technical training languages aside, the reoccurring problematic of embodiment as a potential unifying concept which may be the key bridging these two disciplines across theory and practice remains at the forefront of this cross-disciplinary provocation and in order to move forward, the next step in this collaborative exchange must be determined.

A move towards transdisciplinarity

As a research effort aimed at drawing connections between disciplines through unifying issues or concepts, transdisciplinarity "takes us beyond disciplines by weaving a new kind of knowledge" (Nicolescu, 1997, p. 12–14). The prefix 'trans-' indicates that which is at once between, across, and beyond all disciplines: "its goal is the understanding of the present world, one of the imperatives of which is the unity of knowledge" (Nicolescu, 1997). As a founding member of the Embodied Cognition, Acting, and Performance Symposium at AISB, I entered this new research community as a participant within an exchange of disciplines which aimed to promote interdisciplinary discourse and practice. But this community of researchers and practitioners notably began with an initial and hopeful call for a shift from the interdisciplinary to the transdisciplinary – a move in which performance, and specifically actor training, might serve as a valuable partner to the embodied cognition research programme in undertaking a forward momentum within the development of our shared research and practice towards newly formed models of research and practice. As organisers of this symposium and its corresponding community of researchers, how we approach the concept and practice of embodiment has been explored as a unifying mode of enquiry. The transdisciplinary potential of this enquiry is evident within many of the contributions to this special edition and is indicative of the three-year research journey that many members of this community began together back in 2014 when we first proposed a space to explore the interrelationships between cognitive science, acting, and performance. If there is one position that we share, it may be an intensifying interest in applications cognitive science within performance practices and a growing awareness that embodiment and the enactive approach in cognitive science offers a unique opportunity for a transdisciplinary discourse or practice to explore the shared synergies between these individual disciplinary fields.

Historically, many disciplinary exchanges between actor training and cognitive science have been largely pluridisciplinary, meaning that there was an implied "cooperation between disciplines, without coordination" wherein "compatible areas of knowledge" (Max-Neef, 2005, p. 6), such as action, emotion, and empathy, were integrated on a hierarchical level where cognitive science served as a theoretical method for reinforcing and validating the practice of acting. Furthermore, as a linguistic concept, embodiment has not always featured heavily within the field of actor training, and in that regard it remains a relatively new guest in within our specialist discourse. Unlike cognitive science, the field of actor training does not have an ongoing tradition of engaging with embodiment as an analytic problematic in a way that has advanced us from one stage of theoretical development to the next. (Our central analytic problematic may perhaps be *meaning*. The making of it, the acting of it, the creation of it, the construction of it, the act of it – all possibly bracketed as the presentation and representation of meaning.) However, many of us in the world of performance, and specifically acting and actor training, have intimately worked with and repeatedly lived through the embodied processes and practices of the actor and performer within various framing and practical systems of experiencing within our own disciplines, largely undertaken within a dynamic and unapologetically subjective web of operations, a system of experiencing. It is from this position of embodied practice that many of us make our offerings of synergy to the theories and positionings offered by the embodied research programme.

Where do we go from here?

Within this provocation I have focused on perspectives of embodiment drawn from both embodied cognition and actor training which invite us to view the mind, cognition, and human experience in an increasingly illuminating manner when situated within a cross-disciplinary exchange. The discourses examined provide a brief overview of the ongoing progress that has been made within both disciplinary fields as well as within some current interdisciplinary exchanges, with a larger aim to avoid the privileging of either discipline's mode of theoretical or practical enquiry as hierarchically superior (an issue of concern which is discussed in greater detail within Experience Bryon's contribution to this special edition), and proposes that a crucial contribution may be found through a sustained and unifying exploration of embodiment which aims to heighten our understanding and experience of embodied processes and embodied phenomena through a complex coupling of disciplines which foregrounds the potential to develop this ongoing work further into future transdisciplinary research and practice. In conclusion, I would like to propose some key questions which may give rise to new perspectives and practical undertakings within this cross-disciplinary exchange: How might we utilise or implement a unifying conception of embodiment across, within, and beyond our disciplinary practices? How might this cross-disciplinary discourse support us where others may have failed? To what extent might these findings give way for the emergence of a new discipline or practice through the lens of embodiment? Within the answers to these questions, strong possibilities for trans-disciplinary undertakings are merging within early stages of development and creation, representing the possibility for future fascinating connections derived through advanced research and practice within explorations of embodiment.

Disclosure statement

No potential conflict of interest was reported by the author.

References

Blair, R. (2008). *The actor, image and action: Acting and cognitive neuroscience*. New York, NY: Routledge.

Clark, A. (1997). *Being there: Putting brain, body, and world together again*. Cambridge, MA: MIT Press.
Clark, A. (2010). *Supersizing the mind: Embodiment, action and cognitive extension*. New York, NY: Oxford University Press.
Clark, A. (2012). Embodied, embedded and extended cognition. In K. Frankish & W. M. Ramsey (Eds.), *The Cambridge handbook of cognitive science* (pp. 275–291). New York, NY: Cambridge University Press.

Clark, A. (2016). *Surfing uncertainty: Prediction, action, and the embodied mind*. New York, NY: Oxford University Press.

Gallagher, S. (2005). *How the body shapes the mind*. Oxford: Oxford University Press.

Gallagher, S. (in press). Theory, practice and performance, Connection Science Special Issue on 'Embodied Cognition, Actor Training, and Performance'.

Gillett, J. (2014). *Acting Stanislavski: A practical approach to Stanislavski's approach and legacy*. London: Bloomsbury.

Kemp, R. (2012). *Embodied acting: What neuroscience tells us about performance*. New York, NY: Routledge.

Lakoff, G., & Johnson, M. (1980). *Metaphors we live by*. Chicago, IL: The University of Chicago Press.

Lutterbie, J. (2011). *Toward a general theory of acting*. New York, NY: Palgrave MacMillan.

Mahon, B. Z. (2014). What is embodied about cognition? *Language, Cognition and Neuroscience*. Retrieved from https://caoslab.bcs.rochester.edu/pdf/Mahon_InPress_LCN.pdf

Max-Neef, M.A. (2005). Foundations of transdisciplinarity. *Ecological Economics, 53*, 5–16. Retrieved from http://www.journals.elsevier.com/ecological-economics

McConachie, B. (2008). *Engaging audiences: A cognitive approach to spectating in the theatre*. New York, NY: Palgrave MacMillan.

McConachie, B. (2013). *Theatre and mind*. New York, NY: Palgrave MacMillan.

McConachie, B., & Hart, F. E. (Eds.). (2006). *Performance and cognition: Theatre studies and the cognitive turn*. New York, NY: Routledge.

Nasuto, S. J., & Bishop, J. M. (2011). Of (zombie) mice and animals. In V. C. Muller (Ed.), (2013), *Theory and philosophy of artificial intelligence* (pp. 85–107). SAPERE; Berlin: Springer.

Nicolescu, B. (1997). The transdisciplinary evolution of the university condition for sustainable development. Retrieved from http://ciret-transdisciplinarity.org/bulletin/b12c8.php

Shapiro L. (Ed.). (2014). *The Routledge handbook of embodied cognition*. New York, NY: Routledge.

Sharkey, N. E., & Ziemke, T. (2000). Life, mind and robots – The ins and outs of embodied cognition. In S. Wermter & R. Sun (Eds.), *Hybrid neural systems* (pp. 313–332). Heidelberg: Springer.

Stanislavski, K. (2008). *An actor's work*. New York, NY: Routledge.

Thelan, E. (2000). Grounded in the world: Developmental origins of the embodied mind. *Infancy, 1*, 3–28.

Thompson, E. (2007). *Mind in life: Biology, phenomenology, and the science of mind*. Cambridge, MA: The Belknap Press of Harvard University Press.

Varela, F. J., Thompson, E., & Rosch, E. (1991). *The embodied mind: Cognitive science and human experience*. Cambridge, MA: MIT Press.

Stanislavsky's system as an enactive guide to embodied cognition?

Ysabel Clare

ABSTRACT

This paper presents a model of the structure of subjective experience derived from the work of Konstantin Stanislavsky, and demonstrates its usefulness as a functional framework of enacted cognitive embodiment by using it to articulate his approach to the process of acting. Research into Stanislavsky's training exercises reveals that they evoke a spatial adpositional conceptualisation of experience. When reflected back onto the practice from which it emerges, this situates the choices made by actors as contributing towards the construction of a stable attention field with which they enter into relationship during performance. It is suggested that the resulting template might clarify conceptual distinctions between practices at the unconscious level, and a brief illustrative comparison between Stanislavsky's and Meisner's practices is essayed. A parallel is drawn throughout with the basic principles of embodied cognition, and correlations found with aspects of Dynamic Field Theory and Wilson's notions of "on-" and "off-line" processing.

Towards a conversation

Both acting and embodied cognition address the question of how human beings experience and act in the world: what Varela, Thompson, and Rosch called *enactive embodiment*. As Blair points out in the Preface to her exploration of acting and cognitive neuroscience in 2008:

> Since acting grows out of our biological being, what we are learning about learning and imagination, and the way emotion, reason, and physicality are ultimately inseparable in the brain's structure and function, has significant implications for how we understand what happens when we act. (p. xii)

"What happens when we act" is tied irrevocably to what happens when we *are*: the process of acting offers a rich context from which to explore human experience because the actor has to appear to replicate a human being on stage, and must therefore both know what a human being might be and be able to be one – similar to but different from themselves – despite the distractions of being on stage observed by others.

This paper is intended to initiate a conversational exchange – for as Blair and Cook comment: "It is useful . . . if work in one field is in conversation with another – particularly when both are interested in some of the same questions" (2016, p. 2). However, despite the parallels, it is not my intention to situate the study of acting within the fast developing field of embodied cognition, which has been achieved elsewhere (Blair, 2008; Blair & Cook, 2016; Kemp 2012). Instead, and in the interest of provoking a conversation, the paper presents a model that came directly out of the study of a particular actor training, offering it here because it appears to be an example of embodied cognition in action, providing a how-to guide to being an actor situated in a wider context of a how-to guide to being human.

The Spatial Adpositional Model of Experience (abbreviated as SAME) emerged during exploration of the narrative of exercises in the fictional actor trainings written by acting practitioner Konstantin Stanislavsky. Research comprising detailed textual analysis of these works discovered that via particular sequencing patterns of exercises and student responses, his fictional student Kostya, standing proxy for the reader, incrementally encounters not just his own subjective experience but the (embodied) structure or model within which that experience is encountered, providing him with a broader perspective of all that human experience could be, as well as situating his own experience within the wider context (Clare 2016b). The terms of the model itself are implicitly evoked by the exercises and build into a coherent whole before being appropriated in a particular way so that they can be deliberately manipulated for the purpose of acting.

In this paper, the underlying model, the SAME, is made explicit. Once its terms of reference are outlined, the paper shows that turning it back on the work from which it came evinces a new reading of Stanislavsky's acting process, resituating it as the way he uses the SAME for the purpose of acting: an attentional practice that operates within the SAME and can now be described using its terms. Mapping this attentional practice reveals a template for the process of acting that both *describes Stanislasvky's* embodied practice and offers a fresh perspective on acting *as* an embodied practice. As well as the alignment between the principles of the SAME and embodied cognition, additional correlations between aspects of the model and aspects of embodied cognition have been found, and there are fresh insights into several aspects of Stanislavsky's work.

The SAME and the resulting template therefore appear to offer possibilities for the exploration of other approaches to acting: a brief comparison is made between Stanislavsky and Meisner. The underlying model and the approach to using it for the purpose of acting re-frame Stanislavsky's actor training as an essential training in a language of embodied experiencing, in which the SAME is the primer expressing a generative grammar of enactive embodiment and the template is the syntax of acting.[1]

Basic principles

Bateson suggests that mind is, in a sense, immanent (1972, p. 317). This is a precursor to contemporary views on distributed and environmental cognition. From this perspective, mind predicates body – the perception of the body and by the body is literally essential to it – and environment, in which the body finds itself. As individuals, however, individually experiencing embodiment and situated in the moment in space and time, that experience is inherently subjective, and we still lack a common language to communicate our own experience of embodiment – for the embodied experience *is* the language. Dance *is* the language of dance. Gesture *is* the language of gesture. To teach actors to act, therefore, which requires the understanding and deliberate manipulation of human experience, is inherently challenging: how are we to teach acting, or talk about teaching it, if we cannot speak of subjective experience?

It is the premise of this paper that Stanislavsky's fictional training reveals that certain aspects of embodied experience can, however, be brought into awareness by the individual and mapped using a spatial adpositional framework. This subjectively perceived, relational construct unconsciously structures the organisation of information such as memory, imagination, computation and thought both abstract and literal, and is evidenced in verbal and non-verbal language such as gesture and facial expression. Conversely, that same verbal and non-verbal language reveals specific information about the unconscious structure that informs it, which is rendered visible and readable to those aware of the underlying framework.

Because the individual student is able to articulate their own idiosyncratic patterns within a broader template whose frame of reference is contingent upon the perceptual and sensory capabilities of the human system, this training is both essential and plural. Further, it is commensurate with the ideas of theorists and practitioners from a wide range of disciplines, from Bateson (1972) to Merleau-Ponty (2002) and particularly in the field of embodied cognition. Introducing his book *Embodied acting*, Kemp begins from and therefore elaborates Lakoff and Johnson's "three major findings of cognitive science" (1999, p. 3):

> 1 The mind is inherently embodied ... because physical experience shapes conceptual thought ... 2 Thought is mostly unconscious ... 3 Abstract concepts are largely metaphorical, with the sources of the metaphors originating in our kinaesthetic and perceptual experiences of the material world. These experiences generate cognitive systems that reflect our physical environments and form patterns for higher cognitive activity. (Kemp 2012, p. xvi)

Stanislavsky's training addresses all three of these points: it evokes the embodied mind and demonstrates its circularity by extracting conceptual principles shaped by physical experience before converting them back into physical experience for the purpose of acting; it addresses processes of which we are usually unaware; and the metaphorical concepts that originate in perceptual experience of the material world are situated in relation to the body in space and time in three dimensions. But while Stanislavsky's work fits in with these broader principles on which embodied cognition is based, as the latter field has developed it has become less clear in which area the former might be situated. Aspects of the one appear to correlate only with aspects – but not fully realised theoretical frameworks – of the other. This is reflected in this paper, as correlations are remarked upon but the framework as a whole remains true only to the broadest principles.

Physical theatre practitioner Jacques Lecoq based his practice on these same essential principles. He instinctively believed that there is a language beneath words and gestures – what Lecoq called the "fonds poetiques commun" or common language of expression, and that it emerges from embodied experience of the world (Kemp, 2016). This common language articulates both perception and conception, because as Lakoff and Johnson point out, " ... the conceptual system makes use of important parts of the sensorimotor system that impose crucial conceptual structure" (1999, p. 38). It is this general principle – the conceptual structure derived from sensorimotor experience – that is articulated and rendered in practical form by the SAME.

Behind *An actor's work*

It must be emphasised that this is not a model "from" embodied cognition, applied to the work of Stanislavsky. The SAME framework was extrapolated by this researcher during investigations into the work of Konstantin Stanislavsky (Clare, 2014, 2016a, 2016b). It emerged from a detailed exploration of the narrative of the acting exercises in his fictional training diaries. Having been extrapolated, the model is here presented as an independent entity, as an attempt to articulate a perceptual/conceptual language commensurate with the basic principles of embodied cognition, in other words to provide a grammar of enacted cognition at the processual level.

Konstantin Stanislavsky (1863–1938) was a Russian actor, director, and teacher and the first to set out a systematic acting technique. His work was seminal and remains at the forefront of training and continued study today. Reacting against heightened forms of nineteenth-century theatre such as melodrama, and wanting instead to depict authentic human life on stage, his fundamental belief was that truthful acting came from living through the given circumstances of the part. The problem was that actors did not necessarily know how to do this and had a tendency to "represent" or show themselves off instead of "experience" or "live through". His System was intended to remedy this. Training to use it was all-encompassing and included relaxation, attention, and imagination as well as learning how to divide up the text, find objectives appropriate to both part and actor, and prepare for performance.

However, what is commonly known as Stanislavsky's System actually resists definition. The term is used in different ways by different authors to refer to different aspects of the work, ranging from the whole body of practice to beliefs, strategies, methodology, training, or rehearsal process. Individual commentators even offer multiple interpretations, for example Benedetti in one sentence calls it " . . . an activity and a practice . . . a working method . . . a process" (1989, p. xi). Crucially, Stanislavsky himself said there was no System, only nature, and his work was to get closer to it (Carnicke, 2009, p. 67). Furthermore, the translator's note to *An actor prepares* states unequivocally that "There is no claim made here to actual invention" (2008a, no page number given). This research suggests that what Stanislavsky did invent was a strategy: a systematic way to encounter human process and apply it to acting. He was also the first person to write about training in an accessible way.

First published in 1936, *An actor prepares* (Stanislavski, 2008a) influenced generations of English actors and teachers, and even now continues to sell well. The more recent translation reclaims the original title of *An actor's work* (Stanislavski, 2008c).[2] My research suggests that Stanislavsky was not just the first person to set out a sequence of exercises and a way of working but that he did so in a uniquely compelling way. He addressed the problem of articulating experience and embodied practice by manipulating the narrative form of the text, and the text itself therefore evidences the strategies he used.

An actor's work is fictional. It does not purport to be a "true account", to contain a "model acting course", or be a "how-to" guide. Ostensibly a student diary written by the protagonist Kostya, this imaginary narrative must have been devised for the benefit of the reader, not the student participants, who do not exist, and never did. Stanislavsky's choices about the formulation of that narrative, therefore, are significant and, it turns out, revealing.

Exploring the structure of the narrative using the epistemological constructs of difference, re-iteration, and abduction (an analytical methodology derived specifically for this purpose from the work of Gregory Bateson)[3] revealed intricate underlying patterns including rhetorical structure to chapters, repetition of patterns at micro and macro scales, patterns of success and failure, and regular distribution of subjective and objective perspectives (Clare, 2014, 2016a). Apparently random consequences of practice could now be seen to actually serve the narrative, providing extra information that situates the protagonist Kostya's story within a wider context: human experience itself.

On the face of it, the first part of *An actor's work* addresses *Perezhivanie* (experiencing), while Part II, originally published in 1949 as *Building a character* (2008b) addresses *Voploshchenie* (embodiment). However, in the first text, the students (and the reader) undergo a systematic, incremental encounter with their own unconscious experience, articulated within an embodied frame of reference: both literally and figuratively situating that experience as being embodied in space (and time). This is deep structure, predicated by the surface structure of the exercises, the narrative and the results of the exercises. The students discover their own (embodied) experiencing. Once the model is fully articulated in the individual, students learn how to work and communicate with other subjectively experiencing bodies before applying the model of experience to the process of acting. In the second book, the (embodied) framework of experience evoked in the first part is applied to the experience of embodiment. Now, the body is articulated in the terms of the deep structure. Now, the students experience their own embodiment.[4]

The conceptualisation of embodied human experience evoked in the training diaries takes the form of a coherent experiential model, spatial adpositional in type, and consistent with the experiential realist view of cognitive linguists Lakoff and Johnson (1980, 1999). This model exposes at least some of the rules of metaphoric thinking via structure and organisation. It "maps" the "prenoetic dynamics" (Gallagher, 2016, p.174). Because it functions at the level of structure, it is essentially a meta-model, or model of a model. While superficially different, it also shares structure with other proposed frameworks for understanding human process, such as Pinker's " . . . space as a metaphor for time . . . " (2008, p. 26), Damasio's " . . . spatial and temporal relationships among entities . . . " (2000, p. 318) and his "as-if body loops" (2000, p. 281), and Fauconnier's "space builders" and "space configuration" (1998, p. xxiii). For while these conceptual frameworks appear to vary, at the meta-level they actually share the referents of space, time, and relationship, and can also be represented or conceptualised adpositionally.

The Spatial Adpositional Model of Experience

The spatial adpositional framework is unconscious, predicated on our subjective experience of ourselves as human bodies physically manifest in space and time. Embodied cognition in action, the unconscious structure profoundly affects how we process information and this is evident in behaviour and language. For example, prepositional phrases litter conversation and are informed by and expressed in gesture. Prepositions combine with their referents to indicate semantic relations between subject and context: they are essentially relational. They are also essentially structural and infer three-dimensional perception of the world. This view literally articulates how we construct understanding of our experience: in terms of perceived reality.

Jacob von Uexkull labelled perception of the world, experienced by and through the capacity of species-specific bodies, the umwelt: literally "surround-world" (Brentari, 2015). That is to say, it is inherently embodied because it is biologically limited by the sensory apparatus of the given physical body. Stanislavsky's training implicitly addresses this very subject, teaching the student to contextualise their individual umwelt within a wider framework of the human umwelt: the spatial adpositional umwelt. This both frames the acting process and opens the student's awareness to what is humanly possible. There are two systems here: Stanislavsky's System of acting – or what to do in order to act truthfully – and the system behind the System, referred to by Stanislavsky as the "system of nature".[5] This is the SAME. A description of the model first appears in Clare (2016b), and is cited in the outline below.

The key principle of Stanislavsky's meta-system is that " . . . something is going on inside the human being, and it can be seen and interpreted by others, on the outside". In other words, there is an *inner world* and we are *leaking information* about it. It shares characteristics with the outer world in three ways. First, "experience is mediated by *the senses* – sensory data are transformed and re-presented in internal awareness: a kind of virtual reality of the mind". It is important to note that this is not just about images, and the mind, in this model, is embodied. Furthermore, images are not only visual but fully physically encoded. Second, "the inner virtual reality is *spatial* . . . in three dimensions – a virtual space" in which information is experienced as being comparatively closer or further away, up or down, right or left. All sorts of information is subjectively perceived as stored and/or accessed in this way, from sensory to propositional, processual and abstract. As we refer to this data, we might in turn leak information about it, through *gesture* – indicating relative location (both egocentric and allocentric) via spatial referencing; type of information via type of gesture; and characteristics via literal and metaphoric characteristics of gesture (see, for example, Ekman & Friesen, 1972) – *body language* – indicating response and relationship both literal and metaphoric via major and minor muscle tension patterns – *and facial expression* – indicating response to and relationship with information via eye movements and complex patterns of expression (see, for example, Ekman, 2016).

The third principle is that *relationship* is crucial: " . . . we can shift perspective in relation to information in this virtual space". For example, subjective and objective: "in" and "not in". We can shift between egocentric and allocentric perspectives. This correlates with Merleau-Ponty's distinction between "body schema" – the sense of the body – and "body image" – a representation of the sense of the body in imagic form, and with Wilson's distinction between "on-line" and "off-line" processing (Wilson, 2002, p. 635, see below).

The way information is arranged in Stanislavsky's inner world as evoked by his fictional training, then, is orientational, or adpositional, because it is "orientated in positional relationships to a source in a notional three-dimensional space". In an adpositional model relationship is key. Therefore, in this perceptual model, the

> . . . circumstances of a person's life at any given moment are located perceptually in space, [adpositionally] *around* the body . . . At any given moment, we are experiencing a particular configuration of available thoughts, memories, and feelings: I have called this an *attention field*. (Clare 2016b, original emphasis)

"Time . . . is conceptualized here as a line: a time line." Stanislavsky uses multiple temporal sequences: units, objectives, actions, and bits. We can embody these or not by shifting perspective in relation to the line. On the line is subjective, embodied, experiencing the situation that is located on the line. Off the line is objective, not embodied, observing the line and the situation from a distance.[6] If each moment is visualised as a virtual space around us, the passing of time is perceived literally, in relation to the body, creating a kind of virtual passageway or tunnel. A time tunnel, perhaps.

Stanislavsky's work frequently involves making lines of mental images (2008a, p. 64), and this is often referred to as a two-dimensional projection onto a movie screen. For example, Blair refers to the "image stream" and calls this the "movie-in-the-brain metaphor", pointing out that Stanislavsky was "adamant about the actor's need for a rigorous image-based score" (2008, p. 78). Similarly, Gillett says "We create a series of images *that are projected like a film onto the screen of our mind's eye*" (2007, p. 113, my emphasis). But the SAME shows that the lines are conceptual, and not so much actual lines as *linear sequences*, and that using two-dimensional movie-related analogies might actually be missing a significant distinction in the work. The image sequences might actually be intended to be more like what we would now think of as virtual reality.[7] The three-dimensional attention field – that can be dynamically engaged with in imagination – provides a much richer and more complex and responsive context than a "movie-in-the-brain", a two-dimensional construct to which the actor can only relate as separate. Reframing this as an attention field facilitates full, dynamic, and repeated re-embodiment of a three-dimensional construct.

Within this framework certain phenomena operate, such as emotion memory: I can be minding my own business on my balcony, when the sight of the lantern on the wall reminds me of a ship's lamp and takes me straight back to the Liberty Clipper, and I see exactly what I saw then, experiencing the sights, sounds, and sensations of the sea as I sit (present tense) on deck. This is an example of distortion of present moment experience: I am here, on the balcony; I am also there, on board ship. "There" is now "here". There are other types of perceptual distortion, however, for the actor to contend with, for the inner world is not an accurate representation of the outer world. For example:

> In the 1952 film "Pat and Mike", Katherine Hepburn plays a tennis match with (the real life tennis champion) Gorgeous Gussie Moran. Director George Cukor and Warren Newcombe, in charge of special effects, show us her subjective perspective when her (evidently unsuited) fiancé is watching her: her racket is tiny, while Gussie's is enormous . . . (Clare 2016b)

The ball is minute; the net unsurmountable: her in-the-moment perceptions of object size, distance, and relative position are all distortions of the physical world.

Merleau-Ponty is also interested in distortions of perception. He writes that a female patient had described someone looking at her as though it had struck her physically, and she could not recall or describe the person who had done so: "For her it is not a matter of what happens in the objective world, but of what she encounters, what touches her or strikes her . . . The hallucination is not a perception, but it has the value of reality . . . " (2002, p. 399). He is describing the very type of perceptual distortion that Warren Newcombe illustrated with his special effects. In the work of Lakoff and Johnson, metaphor reveals (leaks) the perceptual distortions that underlie and re-inform experience of the world – metaphors that reflect argument as war, for example, where the perception of the self and the other as "embodied fighters" characterises arguments as "attacking" or "defending", and verbal and non-verbal communication are weapons that have the capacity to "shoot down", "wipe out", or "deflect" (1980, chap. 1).

Being observed is distorting per se. However, it is essential to the nature of performance. Without an audience there is no performance. Unmanaged distortion is therefore a serious problem for the performer. The chemical, biological, or psychological causes of why the awareness of the gaze of the other is distracting are immaterial. What matters is to learn to understand, predict, and manage the actor's own individual distortions in the interest of performance. To avoid this, we must find a way to maintain attention, resist distraction, and respond spontaneously in performance whatever is going on around us. This is fundamental for the actor. Stanislavsky addresses the problem by prescribing a carefully designed and deliberate management of the attention field. Turning the SAME back onto Stanislavsky's work – from which it was derived – reveals the details of how to use it for the purpose of acting.

Generative Relational Attention Field Theory

Tribble refers to "a certain deployment of attentional resources" in which an actor "must banish certain forms of thought and harness others" (2016, p. 138). Stanislavsky tells us exactly how to achieve this. It has been established in the SAME that the circumstances of a person's life are situated around the body in a notional field and perceived adpositionally. The given circumstances of a part must be assembled in the same way, with the same disposition to the actor in performance. The attention is limited to a specific and coherent field. That field is the given circumstances of the part.

If the attention field *is* the given circumstances, then the actor's work is to construct the field. Crucially, structural patterns and consistencies within this field, as well as the actor's responses to them, are apparent to the observer as that information is leaked both verbally and non-verbally.

Stability and consistency is also important. If being observed disrupts the actor's attention, then it takes attention away from the carefully prepared programme of "things to think about" that we have designed for the performance and interrupts the ability to focus. It distorts the perception of both internal and external reality. In order to prevent distortion, we must maintain attention within a stable, pre-prepared, attention field (for Stanislavsky, the given circumstances). Theoretically, once it is stable, an attention field can sustain multiple repetitions, becoming generative and responsive.

The more familiar circles of attention are now re-framed as attentional training devices, and not an end in themselves. They teach the actor to manage attention within the specified field (delineated by focal length), so that they are able to access and maintain the attention field of the given circumstances during preparation and performance.

During preparation the actor moves in and out of the developing attention field to create what they will experience during the play, using "if" to situate themselves "in" the given circumstances, until it is stable and they can repeat it again and again (see Figure 1). During the actual performance, they assume a subjective relationship with the assembled given circumstances so as to experience them dynamically in moment-to-moment perception: embodying them in exactly the same way that they would in their own lives. The actor is "in" or "not in" them, they can tell, and so can others, because it is indicated in their behaviour as they reference the inner world.[8]

Moreover, "The Stanislavsky actor must generate and assemble the given circumstances of the part in the same spatial relationship to their own body as their own given circumstances occur" (Clare 2016b). This creates authentic response, on the premise that information is organised in the attention field according to type, and that type

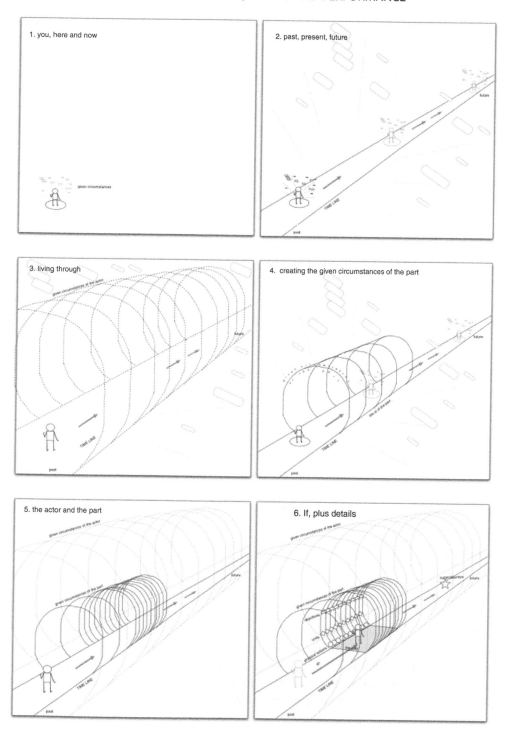

Figure 1. Creating the attention field of the given circumstances.

of information provokes associated or linked type of response (including emotional response).[9]

The attention field as a construct seems to have promise for a broader application. The field itself can vary spatially, temporally, and relationally. It seems to perform a useful function of delineating a range of choices arranged in a distinctive way and pre-programmed during rehearsal to be linked to a sequence of actual events to be engaged with in real time during performance. Because both the relationship and the generative quality exemplified in Stanislavsky's usage of the attention field seem important for the process of acting, it was therefore decided to distinguish this particular use of attention fields as something that might be applied to other acting practice and use these qualities in the name: to call it Generative Relational Attention Field Theory (abbreviated to GRAFT).

Three core principles can be delineated: the underlying principle that human beings unconsciously leak information evidencing process (based on the SAME model); the functional principle of attention fields; and the causes, effects, and uses of perceptual distortion.

The GRAFT proposes that actors prepare for performance by constructing an attention field according to the principles of their particular practice and within the framework of the SAME, even if their practice is to work instinctively. They intentionally create "temporally chained sequences" [10] of attentional acts and possibilities. During the performance actors inevitably leak information about their underlying principles – whatever system or method is employed. Therefore, bringing out the attention fields of different practitioners might make explicit the spatial adpositional differences in the way that they conceptualise and practice acting. This is the very information that is non-verbally leaked during performance via subtleties of body language, gesture, and facial expression.

Now that the model and the template have been outlined, it is possible to show how they might be situated in relation to the field of embodied cognition by identifying some correlations, how they shed light on certain aspects of the work of Stanislavsky himself by reframing them, and how they can be used to make comparisons between practices by using them as a lens through which to re-view the work.

Correlations

The relationship between cognitive science and the work of Stanislavsky has been observed by commentators such as Pitches (2006) and Whyman (2008), and Blair in particular has set out a case for considering Stanislavsky as a pioneer in the understanding of what he called the "human system" (2008, pp. 27–34). The underlying premise of this article is that the unconscious principles of Stanislavsky's actor training allow the student to encounter in practice Lakoff and Johnson's fundamental proposition that "Our conceptual system is grounded in, neurally makes use of, and is crucially shaped by our perceptual and motor systems ... We can only form concepts through the body ... " (1999, p. 555). Their view literally and figuratively *incorporates* the subjective; Stanislavsky shows how to do this in practice for the purpose of acting.

Because Stanislavsky's cognitive architecture is constructed according to the principles of the physical world in which the embodied individual acts, it also has strong correlations with Varela, Thompson, and Rosch's *embodied action*. In similar terms to those of Lakoff and Johnson, Shapiro summarises this approach:

... embodiment involves a deep connection between perception and action. (...) Cognizers make their world, in some sense, as a result of activities that reflect the idiosyncracies of their bodies and perceptual systems. (2011, p. 55)

The SAME could be accounted for in its entirety using this basic proposition. Indeed, its three-dimensional, spatial nature could even be considered to be self-evident, if as Varela, Thompson, and Rosch assert, " ... cognitive structures emerge from the recurrent sensorimotor patterns that enable action to be perceptually guided" (1991, p. 173).[11]

In addition to the fundamental correlation between Stanislavsky's work and these definitions of defining embodied cognition, however, there are three other developments in the field of cognitive science that are worth mentioning in relation to the task of the actor, and whose relevance is highlighted by the SAME. The value of Wilson's "on-" and "off-line" processing as a parallel to associated and dissociated engagement with specific constructs will have become evident during exposition of the model. Also relevant is the work of the Dynamic Field Theory Research Group, and some of the research that has recently taken place on visual–spatial abilities.

First, acting is a process of both pre- and re-situated cognition. If the SAME is a kind of cognitive architecture, articulating a taxonomy of spatial relationship between concepts and emerging out of "on-line" embodied cognition, then the attention field is a selection of perceptual and sensorimotor choices, both unconscious and deliberate, operating within that architecture. The attention field is therefore what Wilson calls a facultative system: "temporary, organized for a particular occasion and disbanded readily ... retain[ing] its identity only so long as the situation and the person's task orientation toward that situation did not change" (2002, p. 630). In Wilson's terms, the Stanislavsky actor deliberately revisits this particular facultative system – the attention field – when they revisit the situation (given circumstances of the part) and their task orientation (subjective/living through). The organisation of the system is relationally distributed between the situation, the person, and the orientation, and is open, in that it responds to its environment during rehearsal and performance.

Wilson usefully highlights the same distinction made by Merleau-Ponty when she notes that the claim that cognition is situated does not always apply, for what she calls "off-line" cognitive activity "is by definition not situated".

... one of the hallmarks of human cognition is that it can take place decoupled from any immediate interaction with the environment. We can lay plans for the future, and think over what has happened in the past. We can entertain counterfactuals to consider what might have happened if circumstances had been different. We can construct mental representations of situations we have never experienced, based purely on linguistic output from others. ... our ability to form mental representations about things that are remote in time and space ... is arguably the sine qua non of human thought ... . (2002, p. 626)

This "ability to form mental representations about things that are remote in time and space ... " is not only the sine qua non of human thought, it is exactly what the actor does in preparation for performance: the sine qua non of acting.

While the preparation of the actor to perform is necessarily decoupled from the situation of performance because they are separated in time, however, this type of what Wilson calls "off-line" cognition is not necessarily decoupled from the embodied self. Mental processing, including the use of imagery, is not only visual, and "images" are not necessarily "image-like". She points out that sensorimotor systems are implicated in mental imagery, memory, and reasoning: for example "Phenomenologically, recalling an episodic memory has a quality of 'reliving,' with all the attendant visual, kinesthetic, and spatial impressions" (2002, p. 633). Preparation for a role, then, is an example of " . . . the use of bodily resources for cognitive purposes not directly linked to the situation" (2002, p. 629).

Second, Dynamic Field Theory works towards a new and intentionally integrated theory of cognition. Spencer and Schoner write in the introduction to the work of the DFT Research Group that they are aiming:

> Toward a unified theory of cognitive dynamics . . . DFT provides an *embodied* account, that is, neural processes are grounded in sensory and motor processes that are anchored on a body situated in a physical environment. . . . we are pursuing a general theory that spans perception, action, and cognition. . . . carrying forward a set of common principles as we move from lower- to higher-level cognition. (2015, pp. xiii–xiv)

In this Primer, the Group discusses a variety of aspects of cognitive dynamics that could be relevant to the consideration of the process of acting. This paper has raised several conceptual differences that might respond to such analysis. The Group outlines different types of attention fields (spatial attention fields, scene attention fields, feature attention fields, transformation attention fields, contrast fields, and retinal fields) within which attentional foregrounding, hills and peaks of activation, and sequential transitions occur. Although these are short-term attention fields, they can be related to the constructed attention field of the actor, a long-term, artificially sustained field with a complex contextual function. It should perhaps be noted that all these fields operate within the parameters of the SAME and are differentiated according to its terms. They are all aspects of the visual experience of a three-dimensional environment and can be mapped in relation to each other in it.

Other potentially relevant aspects of DFT include descriptions of working memory fields as feature, spatial, or scene, and the distinction made between sequential versus parallel processing modes. In a chapter on "Integrating perception-action with cognition" (pp. 197–226), Schneegans, Spencer, and Schoner (2015) address the attention field and working memory patterns of individuals in relation to objects in the real world – it would be extremely useful to extend this to imagined objects and the conceptual world within which actors function and construct the lives of their parts over time. DFT apparently offers several promising avenues for investigation of the process of acting.

Third, a rather different prospect is offered by the exploration of different types of processing abilities. The process of the transformation of sensory-based information into recalled information is highly important for actors (this was the first principle of the SAME). While researching the ability to recall and represent navigational routes, Blajenkova, Motes, and Kozhevnikov found that

> . . . individual differences in environmental representations are related to individual differences in visual-spatial processing abilities that high visual-spatial abilities may lead navigators to produce survey-type representations after only a single exposure to a route. (2005, p. 108)

It follows that if spatial abilities affect the type of representations formed, and Stanislavsky's actor must form clear representations of imagined temporospatial environments, then selecting students who might be expected to do well within this framework means identifying and picking those who have strong visuo-spatial abilities during the audition process. Similar criteria might apply to other acting systems and methodologies. For example, Kozhevnikov, Kosslyn, and Shephard (2005) show how the distinction between the processing of object properties and spatial properties in the visual system also pertains in mental imagery and that there is no correlation between object and spatial ability in individuals. "The results also indicate that object visualisers encode and process images holistically, as a single perceptual unit, whereas spatial visualisers generate and process images analytically, part by part" (2005, p. 710). Could there be a correlation between the Chekhov actor, operating holistically (Chekhov, 2002), and object visualisers? Would this contrast with a similar correlation between the spatial visualisers and the Stanislavsky System that predicates the ability to use space to organise time? Does the SAME only resonate with visuo-spatial thinkers or is it equally recognisable by object visualisers?

In addition, it may be possible to ascertain whether students perceived by teachers to be "good at acting" might score highly on visuo-spatial abilities if the Stanislavsky System is preferred, and whether different conservatoires are already – knowingly or unknowingly – selecting students who have different abilities, indicating a particular cognitive style, using intuition or evidence in body language.

Reframes

As well as raising points about acting in general, using the model and the template to re-articulate aspects of Stanislavsky's practice highlights several possible shifts or changes in perspective on his own work.

First, as well as re-situating the whole System within the SAME cognitive architecture and the given circumstances as an attention field, the spatial adpositional model provides a coherent framework that *integrates* Stanislavsky's work because it situates the embodied actor within the attention field, bringing all the actor's embodied experience – which includes their embodied use of all aspects of the System – with them. The system is no longer fragmented because everything is related to the body of the actor as the source of the SAME and the attention field. Thus once the attention field is fully realised, it becomes clear how "if" is not the only way to access the given circumstances: each aspect of the System is related to this central process and can play a part in triggering requisite engagement with the attention field. The framework allows the actor to discover, develop, and deliberately use the triggers that work for them.

Second, there is a linguistic difficulty with the verb "to act", and related terms such as "action" and "enact". This can lead to opaque statements such as "the actor has to act".[12] Now, what the actor has to do (action) can be reframed using the SAME as meaning "the actor has to fully engage with a generative, relational attention field". This seems much more specific, understandable, achievable, and measurable.

Third, it has been claimed that Stanislavsky's book potentiates in its first part the embodied self in relationship with space and time, and in its second the experienced body in relationship with space and time. The phrases *embodied experiencing* and *experiencing embodiment* express the inextricable relationship between the two terms, and using them avoids the separating effect of saying "experiencing *and* embodiment". It circumvents the false polarisation. Furthermore, as well as situating the dynamic body in the context it also situates the body as experiential mediator and qualifies the relationship.

Somewhat tangentially, the SAME can also be used to shed light on conceptual structures. For example, Stevens describes meshed expertise as " … a kind of vertical integration between the low-order flow of embodied coping . . . and higher-order, more reflective cognitive aspects" (Stevens, 2016, p. 178). Since he is referring to preparation (higher order) and performance (low-order flow), it provides a parallel with Wilson's online and off-line processing cited earlier (2002, p. 635) pertinent to the actor's preparatory relationship with the timeline, eventually situated within the wider field of the given circumstances. The vocabulary used infers a vertical rather than horizontal organisation of the relationship, which "makes sense" because this more easily allows for simultaneous rather than alternative function. This distinction fits with a model in which the temporal is mapped horizontally and distinctions made using spatial sorting on the horizontal plane. Verticality therefore appears to correlate with the feasibility of integration.[13]

A comparison

Finally, if the SAME does articulate the unconscious terms of some kind of naturally occurring spatial adpositional framework, an explicit version of Lecoq's fonds poetiques commun, then it might be possible to use it, and the GRAFT template, to examine other acting practices. To that end, a brief sample comparison is now undertaken between the underlying principles of Stanislavsky and Meisner.

Sanford Meisner (1905–1997) left the Group Theatre, of whom he was a founder member along with Strasberg, Harold Clurman, and Cheryl Crawford, because he did not agree with Strasberg's emphasis on emotional memory. He observed: "Affective memory has a tendency to make actors more introverted . . . many actors are *inherently* introverted. Introverted actors tend to retreat into their thoughts, where they can't react fully to what goes on around them" (Esper & Dimarco, 2008, p. 215).

Meisner's approach "emphasized *doing* and *reacting* as the key to liveness and spontaneity on stage" (Gordon, 2006, p. 87, original emphasis). His fundamental belief was that emotional truth comes from allowing instinctive response to observed reality in the moment, but the problem is that this impulse is habitually inhibited, because thinking prevents access to instinct: we both conceal ourselves and prevent spontaneous response. Meisner worked towards the "reality of doing": the actor's instinctive response in the moment: the "pinch and the ouch". In his training, students repeatedly focus attention on observing and responding to a scene partner in the famous "repetition exercise", eliminating difficulties and inhibitions as they emerge. In terms of the GRAFT, the result is the ability to focus deliberately within an attention field that includes self and other, and to respond instinctively to stimuli within that field.[14]

What differences are there between the construction of Stanislavsky's and Meisner's attention fields during preparation? Using Wilson's "on-line" and "off-line" designations, one might suppose that the performance would take place "on-line", while the preparation would be "off-line". However, there are differences here.

Stanislavsky's attention field consists of the given circumstances (see Figure 2), including physical reality, with the exception of the audience (the actor imagines a "fourth wall" and the attention field therefore does not accommodate the presence of the audience). The actor is subjectively situated in the field using "if": asking them the question "what would you do 'if' you were living through these given circumstances?" This situates choices made – as well as the performance – as being made both "on-line" and "on *the* line". The objective is

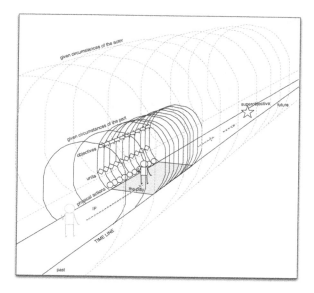

Figure 2. Stanislavsky's attention field: the given circumstances and 'if'.

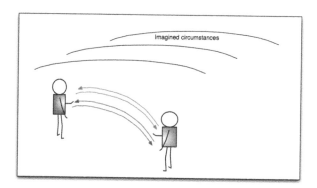

Figure 3. Meisner's attention field: the other.

always within awareness both visual and kinaesthetic. There is a sense of forward momentum as the actor moves psychophysically towards the objective. The character does not
exist as a separate entity at any point in the process.

Meisner's attention field does feature imaginary circumstances, but the Meisner actor
lives not through but *under* these *imagined* circumstances: there is a difference between
living through and living under. However, these circumstances recede in the interest of
consistent focus on experiencing relationships in the immediate present (see Figure 3).
This attentional sub-field is a dynamic circular process situating the to and fro relationship between on stage partners. It would appear that the actor prepares almost continually
"on-line", although there is some brief textual analysis that takes place "off-line" during the
process. Like Stanislavsky there is, conceptually speaking, no *character* during the process
or in performance.

Comparing the two fields, Stanislavsky's attention field is a linear representation – a perceptual time tunnel – and a subjective perspective to it: no character. Meisner's attention

field is dual but simultaneous: the dynamic relationship with the other within a larger attention field of imaginary circumstances. Like Stanislavsky the actor is not separate from the character but subjectively living in the field.

When they are visualised in three dimensions, these practices result in a different psychophysical direction or energy flow in performance and this can also be compared (see Figure 4). The Stanislavsky actor moves, metaphorically speaking, forward towards the objective, situated in front of them and to which they are drawn by a visual-kinaesthetic connection. The energy of Meisner's actor flows back and forth between self and other. "Meisner's fundamental principle [is that] the other actor is the determinant of your responses and behaviour" (Moseley, 2012, p. 171). Both can be expressed gesturally, and not just visualised – the diagram expresses an embodied engagement with an intangible energy – visualisation helps to locate and specify it in a kind of visual-kinaesthetic synaesthesia. Making the gesture informs understanding of the practice.

Different modes of conceptual progression through the temporally chained sequence of events that is the play are taken: Stanislavsky's actor lives *through the given circumstances* and Meisner's lives *under imagined circumstances*. Within that temporal frame,

Stanislavsky

Psychophysical direction

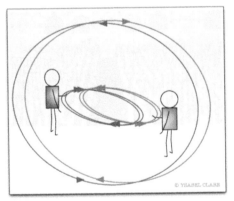

Meisner

Figure 4. Comparison of psychophysical direction.

The actor's relationship with time during performance

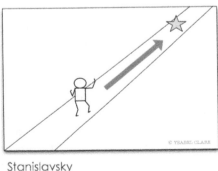

Stanislavsky   Meisner

Figure 5. Comparison of relationship with time during performance.

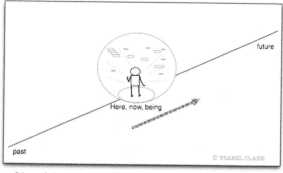

Stanislavsky

Distortion

Meisner

Figure 6. Comparison of distortion.

Stanislavsky's actor moves *towards* objectives, progressing *through* time, while Meisner's appears to *remain* in the same, stable, conceptual location with time passing (see Figure 5).

Given the importance of perceptual distortion for the use of the GRAFT, it is interesting to compare this too (see Figure 6). Stanislavsky's process aims for no distortion in cause (sensation), representation (image), or effect (perception). Meisner, like Stanislavsky, appears to focus on undistorted image and perception, but the attention field is actually distorted deliberately to include the other. For Meisner, the other is part of the environment and arguably, therefore, an integral part of the (distributed) embodied self.

Conclusions

This research situates Stanislavsky's actor training as a training in conceptualist schematic mapping that accords with the work of Lakoff and Johnson emerging originally out of the field of psycholinguistics. Because Stanislavsky's work comprises a whole system of training, rehearsal and performance practices that use his experience of being human in order to act truthfully on stage, it is perhaps unsurprising that while some correlations relating to specifics have been found, the underlying model correlates most closely with general principles of embodied cognition rather than falling into a particular or more recent theoretical framework.

The article began by stating the aim of beginning a conversation and does not therefore aim to conclude one. However, by laying out the parity between the basic principles of embodied cognition and the SAME, examining other more specific correlations, and showing how the template drawn from the application of the model works both in re-presenting Stanislavsky's work and as a potential medium for comparisons between practices, it is hoped that a case has been made to justify its inclusion in the field and in the conversation between acting practice and embodied cognition.

The paper has offered an articulation of a meta-model of human process, derived from the work of Stanislavsky, and supplemented with a new perspective on attentional management in acting practice. The principles of the framework have themselves reflected back onto Stanislavsky's work, providing a new way to articulate it in specific sensory and perceptual terms, and use those terms to venture an initial comparison with other models of acting practice.[15]

Is this SAME framework, a model derived from the underlying principles of Stanislavsky's System, really an enactive guide to a subjective model of embodied cognition?

What would such a guide do? It would make its terms – which would have to match those of embodied cognition – explicit, lay out a map of the contextual framework, articulate the relationship between map and subject, and show how to operate within the framework and to manipulate it for specific purposes.

The SAME does appear to provide an abstract framework based on sensorimotor and perceptual experience of the world, in which Stanislavsky's Mindful Actor (Clare, 2015) can be seen to be experiencing embodiment and embodying experience. The terms are explicit. They are based on sensorimotor and perceptual experience of the body in space and time. They do represent a conceptual model of embodied experience. The GRAFT makes it enactive: it shows how to dynamically engage with the SAME so that, situated HERE and NOW, and BEING, Stanislavsky's actor is literally "in" the moment – experiencing unmediated by distortion: situated *within* the attention field of the given circumstances. If that is what an enactive guide to embodied experiencing would do, then the model and template together are just that.

Stanislavsky constantly re-iterates throughout *An actor's work* that this work is psychophysical.[16] He was known to have read William James, and as Wilson (2002, p. 625) points out, James was one of the "early sources" of the movement in cognitive science away from the idea of "the mind as an abstract information processor" and towards "the idea that the mind must be understood in the context of its relationship to a physical body that interacts with the world". Although he did not "speak" embodied cognition, he does seem to have found another way to put it into practice.

As for this research, limitations are acknowledged. However, the fact that it takes a subjective view could be an advantage when working with actors. Stanislavsky's acting practice is *about* subjectivity. If the model is easily understandable and recognisable in an actor's experience, then it is useful to them. How many actors would be willing and able to understand and extrapolate information from the Primer on Dynamic Field Theory and use it in practice? The SAME and GRAFT can be taught explicitly or implicitly, separate from other practices or alongside, informing them. They are usable and accessible, based as they are on subjectively recognisable principles of embodied cognition in action as experienced by – at least some – individual human beings. As a teacher of acting, I am interested in what works.

As a researcher, I am interested in what comes next, out of these new and untried models. The models have potential as tools for a more thorough investigation of acting practice, to make distinctions between conceptualisations of acting practices, and to investigate how processing preferences might affect innate acting ability. Are these principles evident in the behaviour or observed body of the actor acting? Can they be used to explore exactly how – or whether – the *performance* of, say, a Meisner actor differs from that of a Stanislavsky actor, and whether the differences are observable on stage? There are also possibilities emerging from DFT, and in the wider field, imaging of conceptual structuring, gesture, and eye movements.

Certainly, more research is certainly needed before any claims could be made as to whether these models are "true", "universal", or "scientific". But, if they are useful, and recognisable, as models of subjective experience, then they are usable by subjectively experiencing actors. And if the work of an acting teacher or director is to help the actor to leak the right information, then for now, these models might have something to contribute to that task.

Notes

1. Syntax: noun. "1. The way in which linguistic elements (as words) are put together to form constituents (as phrases or clauses). 2. A connected or orderly system: harmonious arrangement of parts or elements" (Merriam-Webster, 2016). http://www.merriam-webster.com/dictionary/syntax.
2. Different commentators spell the name differently. My own preference is to follow Sharon Marie Carnicke and use the Russian -y ending. Others use the -i ending.
3. "The fundamental relation is *difference*. These basic relational distinctions are, Bateson asserted, the basis of everything from the simple cell division that results in human life to the most complex creative work such as Balinese art" (Clare, 2016b).
4. Paradoxically, focus on Stanislavsky's "inner" world – *Perezhivanie* – is articulated in terms of the world exterior to the body, and focus on the "outer" world – *Voploshchenie* – is actually on the interior.
5. There is also a third system – the system of training that allows students to discover both the System of acting and the system behind the System (Clare 2016b).
6. It is important to distinguish between Wilson's vocabulary (from computing) – "on-line" and "off-line" – and the terminology used here – "on *the* line" and "off *the* line" – which states the subject's relationship to the visualised temporal sequence that comprises the embodied conceptualisation of time. While they actually denote the same thing, they comprise different perspectives, since the underlying metaphor is different.
7. In the chapter on imagination, exercises evoke active and passive engagement with mental images (2008a, pp. 57–58), being present in the imagined situation (pp. 60–63), and three points of view in relation to the image stream: active participation, watching as though present, watching as though not present.
8. This can be checked subjectively by comparing the eye movements and relational gestures present when thinking or talking about an imagined event as though you are actually in the situation (seeing the environment around you, the ground beneath your feet, the bodily sensations, as they are in that context) with seeing yourself in that situation (including the sense of yourself, but firmly situated in the here and now). This difference is also illustrated in language: there is a contemporary tendency to relate events in a colloquial "historic present", re-enacting ("I was, like, 'don't you talk to me like that'") instead of reporting speech and emotion ("I was very annoyed and told her so").

9. For example, identifying the relative disposition (spatial relationship) and characteristics of information that provokes feelings of abandonment and situating imagined given circumstances here with the same characteristics will provoke those feelings when those given circumstances are accessed. This provides a new reading of the term "analogous".

10. Gallese uses this phrase when writing about mirror neurons and the planning and execution of "goal-related motor acts"': these comprise " . . . intentional 'action sentences', that is, temporally chained sequences of motor acts properly assembled to accomplish a more distal goal-state" (2009, p. 168). If parietal mirror neurons code the "overall action intention", then perhaps actors are exploiting this ability on a larger scale. In these terms, the actor's constructed attention field is a chained sequence of intentional "action sentences"', that lasts the duration of the performance.

11. The very use of the word "structure" indicates the conceptual relationship between the sensorimotor patterns and the context in which they occur: space and time. Cognitive structures are *structures*, which is to say experienced in spatial, relational terms.

12. Within the System it can be used to designate an objective or task, the *action* that is executed in order to achieve the task, a physical action, or the basic principle of what the actor has to do, depending on the version of his work being used.

13. It does not presuppose it, because while vertical, Dreyfus's conceptual model (of the edifice of knowledge) does not appear to allow for simultaneity but invokes alternative location within it. Top-down and bottom-up processing models allow connection on the vertical plane using direction. The linguistic framing of cognitive architectures is inherently revealing only if it is considered as related to the experiencing body.

14. My interpretation is based on training with Scott Williams, who himself trained with Meisner in the 1970s. Scott noted the lack of critical analysis on his work, and attributed it to the difficulty of explaining what Meisner was doing objectively. Nick Moseley's recent book *Meisner in practice* (2012) talks the reader through the exercises.

15. Extended further, they afford a view of history as an encounter with time, geography with space, and maths as a conceptual path-setter for abstract thought processes.

16. For example: " . . . in every physical action there's something psychological, and there's something physical in every psychological action" (2008c, p. 180).

Disclosure statement

No potential conflict of interest was reported by the author.

References

Bateson, G. (1972). *Steps to an ecology of mind: A revolutionary approach to man's understanding of himself*. New York, NY: Ballantine Books.

Benedetti, J. (1989). *Stanislavski: An introduction*. London: Methuen.

Blair, R. (2008). *The actor, image, and action: Acting and cognitive neuroscience*. London: Routledge.

Blair, R., & Cook, A. (Eds.). (2016). *Theatre, performance and cognition: Languages, bodies and ecologies*. London: Bloomsbury.

Blajenkova, O., Motes, M. A., & Kozhevnikov, M. (2005). Individual differences in the representations of novel environments. *Journal of Environmental Psychology, 25*, 97–109.

Brentari, C. (2015). *Jakob von Uexkull: The discovery of the umwelt between biosemiotics and theoretical biology*. Dordrecht: Springer.

Carnicke, S. M. (2009). *Stanislavsky in focus*. London: Routledge.

Chekhov, M. (2002). *To the actor: On the technique of acting*. London: Routledge.

Clare, Y. (2014). *A study of the structure of subjective experience in Stanislavsky's 'an actor prepares'* (Unpublished doctoral thesis). Goldsmith's, University of London.

Clare, Y. (2015, April). *Stanislavsky's mindful actor: The system as a guide to experiencing embodiment*. Paper presented at AISB Convention, University of Kent, Canterbury.

Clare, Y. (2016a) Stanislavsky's quest for the ideal actor: The system as socratic encounter. *Theatre, Dance and Performance Training, 7*(2), 148–164. doi:10.1080/19443927.2016.1179668

Clare, Y. (2016b). A system behind the system: But is it Stanislavski? *Stanislavski Studies*. doi:10.1080/20567790.2016.1234018

Cukor, D. (Director). (1952). *Pat and mike* [Motion picture]. USA: MGM.

Damasio, A. R. (2000). *The feeling of what happens: Body and emotion in the making of consciousness*. London: Vintage.

Ekman, P. (2016). What scientists who study emotion agree about. *Perspectives on Psychological Science, 11*(1), 31–34.

Ekman, P., & Friesen, W. V. (1972). Hand movements. *Journal of Communication, 22*, 353–374.

Esper, W., & Dimarco, D. (2008). *The actor's art and craft: William Esper teaches the Meisner technique*. New York: Anchor Books.

Fauconnier, G. (1998). *Mental spaces: Aspects of meaning construction in natural language*. Cambridge: Cambridge University Press.

Gallagher, S. (2016). Mapping the prenoetic dynamics of performance. In R. Blair & A. Cook (Eds.), *Theatre, performance and cognition: Languages, bodies and ecologies* (pp. 174–179). London: Bloomsbury.

Gallese, V. (2009). Mirror neurons and the neural exploitation hypothesis: From embodied simulation to social cognition. In J. A. Pineda (Ed.), *Mirror neuron systems: The role of mirroring processes in social cognition* (pp. 163–190). New York, NY: Springer.

Gillett, J. (2007). *Acting on impulse: Reclaiming the Stanislavski approach*. London: Methuen.

Gordon, R. (2006). *The purpose of playing*. Ann Arbor: University of Michigan Press.

Kemp, R. (2012). *Embodied acting: What neuroscience tells us about performance*. London: Routledge.

Kemp, R. (2016, April). *The embodied performance pedagogy of Jacques Lecoq*. Paper presented at AISB Convention, University of Sheffield.

Kozhevnikov, M., Kosslyn, S., & Shephard, J. (2005). Spatial versus object visualisers: A new characterization of visual cognitive style. *Memory and Cognition, 33*(4), 710–726.

Lakoff, G., & Johnson, M. (1980). *Metaphors we live by*. Chicago, IL: University of Chicago Press.

Lakoff, G., & Johnson, M. (1999). *Philosophy in the flesh: The embodied mind and its challenge to western thought*. New York, NY: Basic Books.

Merleau-Ponty, M. (2002). *The phenomenology of perception*. London: Routledge.

Merriam-Webster. (2016). Syntax. Merriam-Webster.com. Web. 28 September 2016. http://www.merriam-webster.com/dictionary/syntax.

Moseley, N. (2012). *Meisner in practice*. London: Nick Hern Books.

Pinker, S. (2008). *The stuff of thought: Language as window into human nature*. London: Penguin.

Pitches, J. (2006). *Science and the Stanislavsky tradition of acting*. London: Routledge.

Schneegans, S., Spencer, J. P., & Schoner, G. (2015). Integrating "what" and "where": Visual working memory for objects in a scene. In G. Schoner, J. P. Spencer, & DFT Research Group (Eds.), *Dynamic thinking: A primer on dynamic field theory* (pp. 197–226). Oxford: Oxford University Press.

Schoner, G., Spencer, J., & DFT Research Group. (Eds.). (2015). *Dynamic thinking: A primer on dynamic field theory*. Oxford: Oxford University Press.

Shapiro, L. (2011). *Embodied cognition*. Abingdon: Routledge.

Stanislavski, K. (2008a). *An actor prepares*. (E. Reynolds Hapgood, Trans.). London: Methuen.

Stanislavski, K. (2008b). *Building a character*. (E. Reynolds Hapgood, Trans.). London: Methuen.

Stanislavski, K. (2008c). *An actor's work: A student's diary*. (J. Benedetti, Trans.). London: Routledge.

Stevens, C. J. (2016). A response: The body in mind. In R. Blair & A. Cook (Eds.). *Theatre, performance and cognition: Languages, bodies and ecologies* (pp. 122–127). London: Bloomsbury.

Tribble, E. B. (2016). Distributed cognition, mindful bodies and the arts of acting. In R. Blair & A. Cook (Eds.). *Theatre, performance and cognition: Languages, bodies and ecologies* (pp. 133–140). London: Bloomsbury.

Varela, F., Thompson, E., & Rosch, E. (1991). *The embodied mind: Cognitive science and human experience*. Cambridge, MA: MIT Press.

Whyman, R. (2008). *The Stanislavsky system of acting: Legacy and influence in modern performance*. Cambridge: Cambridge University Press.

Wilson, M. (2002). Six views of embodied cognition. *Psychonomic Bulletin and Review, 9*(4), 625–636.

Reverse engineering the human: artificial intelligence and acting theory

Donna Soto-Morettini

ABSTRACT

In two separate papers, Artificial Intelligence (AI)/Robotics researcher Guy Hoffman takes as a starting point that actors have been in the business of reverse engineering human behaviour for centuries. In this paper, I follow the similar trajectories of AI and acting theory (AT), looking at three primary questions, in the hope of framing a response to Hoffman's papers: (1) How are the problems of training a human to simulate a fictional human both similar to and different from training a machine to simulate a human? (2) How are the larger questions of AI design and architecture similar to the larger questions that still remain within the area of AT? (3) Is there anything in the work of AI design that might advance the work of acting theorists and practitioners? The paper explores the use of "swarm intelligence" in recent models of both AT and AI, and considers the issues of embodied cognition, and the kinds of intelligence that enhances or inhibits imaginative immersion for the actor, and concludes with a consideration of the ontological questions raised by the trend towards intersubjective, dynamic systems of generative thought in both AT and AI.

> Theatre actors have been staging artificial intelligence for centuries. If one shares the view that intelligence manifests in behaviour, one must wonder what lessons the AI community can draw from a practice that is historically concerned with the infusion of artificial behaviour into such vessels as body and text .... Therefore, acting methodology may hold valuable directives for designers of artificially intelligent systems.

In his paper, *On stage: robots as performers* (2011), human–robot interaction (HRI) specialist, Guy Hoffman takes as a starting point that actors have been in the business of reverse engineering human behaviour for centuries. In other words, actors work from observable behaviour backwards, to discover motivation, intention, desire, etc. Of course an actor cannot consider imagined intentional states without an accompanying consideration of many varied external factors, such as the social/human forces that will affect decisions, character-specific psychology or contextually specific social "display rules" that might govern just how much of a character's "inner state" can or will be expressed. Still, for all this complexity, the actor is in the business of analysing human intelligence and in manifesting intentional states through behaviour, and this makes the area of acting theory[1] (AT) of interest in relation to theories and practice in artificial intelligence (AI).

Specifically, Hoffman narrows his interest in AT down to two areas: continuity and responsiveness. He references acting practitioner/theorists (Stanislavski, Sonia Moore, Michael Chekhov, Augusto Boal, Sanford Meisner) and makes specific recommendations for robotics design based on AT, outlining a number of applications to robotics, including programming human-interactive robots with an "inner monologue" that might lead to more fluid responses, and exploiting "Meisner 'responsiveness'" to interactive robot design to create a more anticipatory response.

In this paper, I want to look at three primary questions:

(1) How are the problems of training a human to simulate a fictional human both similar to and different from training a machine to simulate a human?
(2) How are the larger questions of AI design and architecture similar to the larger questions that still remain within the area AT?
(3) Is there anything in the work of AI design that might advance the work of acting theorists and practitioners?

In order to consider these questions, I'd like to look closely at two areas that Hoffman's brief paper addresses: (1) embodied cognition (psycho-physical unity) and (2) the location of responsiveness/action choice and the problems of 'single agent' design.

The imitation game

Perhaps these days when thinking about the field of AI, most people think of the pioneering work of Alan Turing, whose 1950 article, *Computing machinery and intelligence* opened with "I propose to consider the question: can machines think?" Turing carries on to describe his now well-known "imitation game", which was an early challenge to the design of pure AI. Turing's game is played by a man, a woman and an interrogator who, without seeing or hearing them, must determine which is the man and which the woman. This opening game then leads to his main interest:

> We now ask the question, "What will happen when a machine takes the part of [the man] in this game?" Will the interrogator decide wrongly as often when the game is played like this as he does when the game is played between a man and a woman? These questions replace our original, "Can machines think?" (Turing, 1950, p. 433)

In the 60-plus years since he posed his challenge, this question remains at the heart of the evolving field of AI. But it is the more direct problem that Turing poses here – the relationship between the "real" and the simulated – that has bedevilled actors for centuries: can an actor A convince auditor C that his imitation of Hamlet is 'real'? And perhaps in that sense, we might say that much theatre criticism, and even the experience of watching an actor perform, are forms of Turing's test.

Actors, of course, have a great advantage over robots in playing the imitation game. Being human, they already have a vast store of human experience to draw upon. They move and think and behave in human ways, have immediate access to their own intentional states, can draw quickly on abstract symbolic processing systems, are equipped with natural speech function and the ability to avoid obstacles when moving through space.

Still, when encountering Hoffman's brief paper, I was struck by how many of the things AI designers face are things that still challenge those who are in the business of directing or training actors. It is striking how often the way in which we describe an unconvincing actor is to say that their work is robotic or has a robotic quality. This sometimes refers to the way in which actors can be physically stiff and uncomfortable in their bodies; sometimes to the ways in which actors seem to be delivering their lines without a requisite (illusionary?) depth of thought behind the delivery, and sometimes it refers to the ways in which a performance can seem 'calculated' or pre-determined. It is common to hear all of these types of performance described as 'robotic'. And although it may be no more than an old actor's joke to recall the experienced actor's advice to the novice: "don't bump into the scenery", it still reminds us of the way in which learning actors face many of the AI designer's problems.

Conversely, there are critical accounts of how actual robots have gone wrong, and these descriptions may remind us of the way that acting teachers often describe the difficulties their students are having. A case in point might be the description (Brighton & Selina, 2003) of William Gray Walter's robot, Elsie:

- "She did not have knowledge of where she was or where she was going
- She was not programmed to achieve any goals
- She had little or no cognitive capacity." (p. 68)

Most actors will recognise in this short list the basics of Stanislavski's critique of the acting he wished to transform with his ideas, and his emphasis on the importance for individual actors to focus their preparation by paying close attention to their character's objectives, given circumstances, and the development of the character's thought process. Consequently, if it is the case that we describe bad actors as robotic, then perhaps under-performing robots may be described as bad actors.

Evolving theories of AI and robotic human simulation

AI has evolved much in regard to theories about the relationship between brain, body and mind, and it is fair to say that what has been come to be called GOFAI (Good Old Fashioned Artificial Intelligence) was largely concerned with pure AI. Turing's interest was in whether machines could think, and thinking in terms of the imitation game was about a computational intelligence. Of course here is where all the challenges for AI begin, because there are so many ways of defining intelligence and ways of talking about what AI means in relation to creating artificial forms of intelligence.

Without straying too far from our interests, I think it is important to note the distinction between 'strong' and 'weak' forms of AI research. Strong AI more or less holds the opinion that humans are elaborate computers, and that if one could crack the codes within that elaborate structure, and identify its constituent parts, then human consciousness – thoughts, feelings, emotions – could be wholly replicated. In that sense, 'strong AI' is probably of some interest to the actor, since we could argue that the labour expended by the actor in rehearsal – analysing the components of and the influences on Macbeth's behaviour – allows the actor to replicate/simulate the human consciousness of Macbeth. That replicated/simulated consciousness is, of course, metaphorically parasitic[2] on the actor's own human consciousness, but it is still a process of replication/simulation. Always cognisant of ontological difficulties here (and which I will address in conclusion), I would like to pose some questions arising in terms of the actor's working conceptions of intelligence and ask: does this suggest that actors have some sympathy with the strong AI community's belief that humans are elaborate biological, computational entities, whose behaviour is *generated* by complex (but ultimately replicable/comprehensible) thought processes? Do actors balance their representations of human behaviour on a belief that by understanding and identifying certain intelligent components of behaviour we execute decisions that replicate the human behaviour of a character other than our own character? Is it the case that we disaggregate human behaviour (reverse-engineer the observables), following links back to the unobservable, discrete intentional states and desires and then create an executable cognitive programme? While many make the case that Stanislavski's early theories were largely concerned with this kind of activity,[3] we know that even Stanislavski himself recognised the limitations of this 'top-down' model. And while there are varieties of AI research that follow this 'top-down' model, many evolving theories of AI are working in the other direction.

The limits of 'top-down' modelling have become as clear to AI researchers as it did to Stanislavski in his later writings, and the function of the body as an element of cognitive processes has become an area of increased interest both in AI and AT. Much current AI is concerned with 'bottom-up' models that proceed from the idea that in order to create a model of human cognition, it is necessary to think in terms of how humans produce action in response to specific environments. This is one area where the relationship between AI and AT grows particularly interesting, and we can follow the theories simultaneously.

Traditionally, most AI research has worked from a SENSE → THINK → ACT (S-T-A) model: a linear paradigm of perceptual sense/sensor → leading to computational programme → leading to choice of motor action. It is fair to say that traditional (Stanislavski) AT has worked in this way too: perceptual information about environment and given circumstances → leading to a cognitive process that considers choices → leading to a specific action. But both AI and AT have developed models that have moved away from S-T-A to reconsider the complex relationship between each part of this tripartite linear model, resulting in a 'bottom-up' approach in both areas. This relocation of interest has occurred alongside (or is perhaps a result of) the growth of interest in the notion of embodied cognition, or a re-evaluation of the relationship between action–perception systems and semantic processing.

Hoffman (2012) explains the way that a bottom-up process operates in his work in robotics:

> [T]he role of action and motor execution in robotics has traditionally been viewed as a passive "client" of a central decision-making process, and as such at the receiving end of the data and control flow in robotic systems. Even in so-called Acting Perception frameworks (Aloimonos, 1993), the influence of action on perception is mediated through the agent changing its surroundings or perspective on the world, and not by internal processing pathways. Instead, we suggest that action can affect perception and cognition in interactive robots in the form of symmetrical action-perception activation networks. In such networks, perceptions exert an influence on higher level associations, leading to potential action selection, but are also conversely biased through active motor activity. (p. 5)

Hoffman's description suggests that perception (which belongs, traditionally, to the first part of SENSE → THINK → ACT)[4] is not part of a discrete, tripartite model, but is permeable and subject to *bias* through motor activity. This idea emerges from relatively new ways to conceive the ACT part of the S-T-A formula, and more specifically from recasting action itself as something other than "passive client". The subsequent challenges in attempting to locate, precisely, the locus of thought/action is as interesting and critical for AI as it is for AT. For AI, and for Hoffman in particular, the question is how to theorise and realise the complex relationship between the sensory/perceptual and action choice.

That complex relationship may be seen differently, of course, depending on the role of THINK in our linear structure, particularly since many branches of cognitive science and AI research significantly devalue (or at least reformulate) the ways in which the traditional top-down model has worked. Hoffman's embodied alternative rests on a seminal article by Brooks (1991), in which Brooks lays out his belief that

> human level intelligence is too complex and little understood to be correctly decomposed into the right subpieces at the moment, and that even if we knew the subpieces we still wouldn't know the right interfaces between them. Furthermore, we will never understand how to decompose human level intelligence until we've had a lot of practice with simpler level intelligences. (p. 140)

Concerned largely with "low-level behaviours (such as object avoidance, walking dynamics, and so forth)", Brooks proposed looking to insects and other simple organisms for inspiration, and, as Hoffman points out (2012), for "growing" intelligence as an emergent property of increasingly complex systems. This emergent intelligence from complex interactive systems seems to me to lie at the heart of some recent developments in AT, particularly Viewpoints and Suzuki actor training systems, and we will consider this later.

But importantly, Hoffman's reformulation of SENSE → THINK → ACT is entirely concerned with the way in which perception may be biased towards motor activity, and this, in turn, may relate well to what Pulvermüller (2013) has lately proposed as a kind of "integrative-neuromechanistic explanation of why both sensorimotor and multimodal areas of the human brain differently contribute to specific facets of meaning and concepts" (p. 86). Pulvermüller's influential paper looks very specifically at research into the ways that "resources in cortical motor systems engaged by complex body-part-specific movements are necessary for processing of semantically congruent action words" (p. 102). In the studies that Pulvermüller refers to, it was demonstrated that involving, for example, the arms or legs in complex movement patterns resulted in some memory impairment of arm- or leg-related words. This suggests that the modalities required to process the complex movement itself created a deficit in the action-language processing, and this is turn has significant influence on the way that we see the relationship between action–perception and semantic processing. Ultimately, perhaps, we must accept the limitations of our linear model and consider the relationship between action, perception and cognition to be more accurately illustrated as:

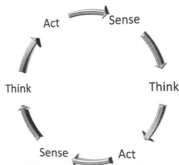

The complex questions surrounding the ways in which we can conceptualise the workings of embodied cognition are as challenging for acting theorists as they are for those involved in the area of AI, and raise a number of questions – only some of which can be answered by reference to scientific literature. I would suggest that we need to think of embodied cognition in very specific ways with regard to AT, because it is one thing to acknowledge the interwoven complexity of perception/cognition, but that acknowledgment does not suggest a separate, 'bodily cognitive' process. In other words, there are ways in which we can talk about embodied cognition that is meaningful for actors but we can't, of course, turn to our knee to ask for advice on how to play Hamlet. That is, of course, a simplification, but there are some implied models of embodied cognition in AT that seem to suggest that there is a kind of brute, unmediated intelligence that inheres in the body and that if we can access this unmediated bodily intelligence we can create conditions for better, more spontaneous performance. For all their success in terms of training, I think that some contemporary acting training systems are focused somewhat in this way, and I want to look specifically at Anne Bogart and Tina Landau's Viewpoints[5] system and Tadashi Suzuki's actor training system.[6]

Like AI, these versions of AT are tinkering with the many possibilities in reframing a SENSE → THINK → ACT model of human behaviour. Also like AI, these methods represent theories that have evolved from a kind of 'top-down' early Stanislavskian model (which, as we have noted, Stanislavski himself amended by stressing the importance of a psycho-physical approach to the analysis and playing of a role), to contemporary 'bottom-up', action/physically based training. In both systems, actors work first from the physical body in a very specific physical environment, and the general aim of both is towards redirecting the actor's attention, in the hope of finding greater freedom and expressiveness in performance. The question is, how do such systems do that?

Viewpoints is a combination of a number of ideas from earlier practitioners (drawing particularly on things like Rudolf Laban's efforts or Michael Chekhov's psychological gesture), and they are very clear about the non-intellectual basis of their approach, suggesting that their method is "a tool for discovering action, not from psychology or backstory, but from immediate physical stimuli" (p. 125). The Viewpoints system comprises a set of specific physical exercises and explorations of space, time and environment. It is particularly focused on creating a kind of 'collective consciousness' of creativity that can help the performer to allow inspiration or perhaps subconscious thought to flow freely. Students are advised to keep a "soft focus" in the room, by which they mean visual perception that isn't aligned with an intentional state, such as "want" or "desire", and they describe a situation in which participants can "learn to listen with our entire bodies and see with a sixth sense" (p. 20). Some of the exercises described in the first part of their book are not dissimilar to older training methods whereby actors "mirror" each other's actions, or attempt to "feel" the moment that a whole group will jump into the air, but their system is much more codified and philosophically distinct. The writers, Bogart and Landau, are working towards their stated aim of creating a responsive ensemble which takes precedence over an intellectual, 'single agent' approach to performing. This collective way of working means that "pressure is released from any one person who feels that they have to create in a vacuum. Emphasis is placed on the fact that the piece will be made by and belong to everyone in the ensemble" (p. 122).

Students are advised against expecting any pre-determined outcomes, and are instead encouraged to "let information come" to them, and to let "something occur onstage, rather than making it occur. The source for action and invention comes to us from others and from the physical world around us" (p. 19). The desired state is one in which "when something happens in the room, everybody present can respond instantly by bypassing the frontal lobe of the brain in order to act upon instinct and intuition" (p. 33). In short, I would argue that the system outlined in their book emphasises a '4E' approach to actor training that is embodied (lead by and discovered through physical interaction), embedded within an ensemble process, extended (in the sense that cognitive choices are mutually created and shared), and enactive (in that the locus of all generative thought and action is intersubjective).

Bogart and Landau write in the style of creative artists, and certainly one would not expect to hear them describe their work in the language of philosophy or cognitive science. But perhaps there is some sympathy between their ideas of bypassing the frontal lobe, and the work of those non-representational theorists like Brooks, or Andy Clark, neither of whom work through a centralised system of modelling environments. Brooks, for example, proposes a system of multiple parallel activities that do n'ot rely on any central representation. These multiple activities avoid a "representational bottleneck" which Clark (1998), in turn, describes as an impedance to real-time responses within an immediate physical environment. In his book, *Radical embodied cognitive science* Chemero (2011) lays a philosophical defence for a theory of computational embodied cognition that generates action-oriented representations (a term first used by Clark), which he sees as constituently different from traditional systems that hold representation to be neutral: "Action-oriented representations differ from representations in earlier computationalist theories of mind in that they represent things in a non-neutral way, as geared to an animal's actions, as affordances" (p. 26). Like Bogart & Landau, Chemero sees cognition as ecological and only understandable in terms of action in a specific environment. It is likely that Viewpoints methods have more to do with ecological psychology and "action-oriented" representation than in the direct suppression of thought when they speak of "by-passing". By emphasising the discovery of action as an environmental response, their method is probably better understood as a systematic approach to redirecting attention. That sounds extremely simple, but in practice, redirecting attention in a sustained way can be quite challenging and have surprising results. One finds a similar theme in the writings of Suzuki (1990), who explains that "our psychological and our physical movements do not naturally blend together" (p. 38), which reminds us that theoretical dualism is often located in the ontological assumptions of the worrying theorist, an area I have explored previously (Soto-Morettini, 2010). Suzuki writes extensively in *The Way of Acting* about the importance of the body in space. He is convincing in his idea that actors must direct attention to the body (particularly the feet) and its relation to environment, but of course before we can put his ideas into practice, we must consider the statement that the psychological and the physical do not naturally blend together.

Suzuki makes this statement specifically in the context of contemporary acting practices in relation to the *nō* theatre practice, which he describes as having begun with

> the expulsion of any expression based on psychology and individual personality; it exists on
> a communality that risks no dispersion . . . .In order for the *nō* to have developed in all its

grandeur, there had to lie behind it the existence of a fixed, decidedly communal playing space. (p. 39)

Suzuki's worry mirrors Bogart and Landau's: the individual brain seems to be getting in the way of our need to respond spontaneously within a specific physical environment. Their mutual solution seems to be a relocation of interest from the 'single agent' brain to the emergent happenings from a kind of swarm model of the type advocated by Brooks and others.

But what might AT and AI gain from this turn to swarm modelling? For AI, the larger picture is related to the possibility of building, through multiple layers of parallel activity, a genuinely real-time responsive environmental intelligence. I believe it also represents a way of working towards complexity by practicing with simpler levels of intelligence (Brooks, 1991) as a necessary starting point. What AT gains, and what lies behind the desire to explore in these 'bottom-up' models, is less the kind of afferent/efferent exchange that Hoffman talks about and much more about attempting to help the actor suppress or redirect the thinking brain before it can interfere with ("bottleneck"?) something that feels as if it arises intuitively and spontaneously from the body and the body's experience.

The larger question for AT is whether, by practicing with simpler levels of interaction and re-directed attention (or "bypassing the frontal lobe"), we can ever hope to build the multiple layers of complexity needed to perform Rosalind. And herein lies some irony. The human–robotic Interaction wing of AI is trying to model behaviour that reflects genuine human thinking processes and AT is trying to model behaviour that suppresses, or redirects some of that genuine human thinking process. And yet, they are in some cases both using a similar 'swarm intelligence' model.

Of course, for AT the 'swarm' model is only concerned to suppress or redirect some kinds of thinking and that is the issue. We are in rather value-laden territory here and that means we must come clean (and, I would suggest, become clearer) about the kinds of cognitive activity we worry about in AT, and the ways in which we judge those cognitive activities. To demonstrate this, we need look no further than a quotation from John Lutterbie's excellent book *Towards a general theory of acting* (2011), in which he considers dynamic systems theory to be of use in "resisting the tendency to differentiate between qualities that are seen as valuable (emotional availability) and qualities that are denigrated (intellectualism)" (p. 103).

Lutterbie's reference to denigrated intellectualism reminds us of Viewpoints's desire to bypass the frontal lobe, and immediately poses the question for us: what is "intellectualism" in acting, and in what way is it denigrated? Lutterbie talks about a "binary of intellect and emotion" that arises when interviewing actors about their practice and concludes that "Rational thought needs to be put on hold so that the experience of images and emotional responses can play freely across and through the body . . . .' (p. 5) There is much that can be said about this – perhaps the first is that it is difficult not to intuit here a rewriting of Cartesian dualism (rational/emotional standing in for mind/body) and the second is that this dualism is a prevalent part of the actor's language, most commonly articulated as "being-in-the-moment" (externally focused attention) vs intellectualising about the action (internally focused symbolic/semantic processing).

For both Lutterbie and Viewpoints, when internal rationality or psychology are involved, the result is the inhibition of external spontaneity or intuitiveness. That inhibition disrupts the balance of imagination and 'belief' – both of which are elusive and fundamental qualities of the actor's work.

Being-in-the-moment and the process of imagination

The aim of Viewpoint's practice is in redirecting attention outward, towards environment, creating a stronger connection between empathic physiology and constantly shifting circumstances, thereby allowing the performer to remain spontaneous and "in the moment". But however desirable that idea is (and in a common-sense manner we can see that if a performer can remain wholly in the moment – attending only to the circumstances, adapting and responding organically and seamlessly – a performance is likely to feel spontaneous and fresh), but as many would argue, consciousness is not really structured this way. The defining quality of consciousness for neuroscientist Gerald Edelman is not simply the present, but "the remembered present". In a particularly provocative conclusion to his influential book, he writes: "Consciousness may be seen as the haughty and restless second cousin of morphology. Memory its mistress, perception its somewhat abused wife, logic its housekeeper, and language its poorly paid secretary" (Edelman, 1989). Edelman's point is that consciousness is not, by definition, an attendance to the here-and-now; not "in the moment" without its household retinue, described above. Rather, "recursive activation of neuronal systems allow organisms that act in the moment and in a particular problematic situation, to redeploy patterns of behaviour that remain continuous with past forms" (p. 196).

For philosopher Dennett (1993), the problem of being 'in-the-moment' would require that we define a "high point" of consciousness which, in his view, never comes. Instead, he describes consciousness as a dynamic process, during which we continually revise through "multiple drafts" whatever we are currently in the process of experiencing. In both Edelman and Dennett's metaphors, we can intuit something about the ways in which consciousness not only works synchronically in past–present–future remembrance/anticipation, but also the ways in which natural human thought moves dynamically in various states of informational input, adjusting, responding and acting as environment evolves. This idea has much resonance with Guy Hoffman's suggestion that robot–human interaction could be strengthened by more anticipatory programming, in which robots might begin to respond with only partial information, which they can revise as new information becomes available. Endowing robots with a kind of 'inner monologue' (a term that Hoffman borrows from AT) that constantly monitors environment would allow them to achieve a more fluid interaction than standard command-and-response behaviour:

> A possible implementation is an opportunistic action selection mechanism, in which robot activity is continuous . . . .The robot can, at any point in time, choose to fully produce one of several implied actions. The actual action selection occurs opportunistically based on current perceptual processing (2011, p. 3).

Of course, for the actor, more than just spontaneous, fluid response is required. The actor works within an imagined world and all of the events within that world must be endowed with a plausible simulation of belief. And if the actor's work is largely a labour of imagination, we are faced with some questions: what are the defining the qualities of imagination in practice, and does the practical imagination gain as much through an embodied environmental context as it might in the kind of isolated imaginative immersion that we sustain in reading a novel? These questions are bedevilled by the very fact that, as Kaag (2008) points out, "The imagination is difficult to define. More often than not, it is not defined at all – only invoked as a placeholder by philosophers when they are unable to define particular cognitive processes" (p. 183). In an article drawing heavily on the work of Gerald Edelman (amongst others), and he defines the neurological basis of imagination as resting largely on the "ecological" processes of mirror neurons in terms of action/perception:

> The research on the mirror neuron system is significant in our investigation of the imagination in the sense that it begins to point to a physiological process that allows organisms to be in touch with their local situations, make generalizations from partial observations, and to adapt to their particular circumstance in the continuous flow of inquiry, learning and adaptation. (p. 194)

Kaag's descriptions remind us of the balance between spontaneous response to environment and the intricate "neuronal architecture" at work in the actor's business of replicating a 'parasitic' intelligence. But if Kaag is right about the physiological basis of imagination, then imagination itself works environmentally, and navigating even an imagined environment requires externally directed attention. If this relationship between physiological processes and environment is the key to responding to particular circumstances, either real or imagined, in an immediate and fluid way, then we must admit the importance of training attention to external circumstances for both performers and robots. In a sense, this is a de-centralising move in terms of developing theories of simulating behaviour. The reward of that de-centralising is an environmental, responsive performance that is greater than one might expect from a performance generated through a single-agent approach. In his description of neural circuitry, Kaag deploys the example of jazz musicians who have played together for many years and Edelman uses the same analogy, concluding that the surprising integration heard in a good jazz improvisation is "a kind of mutually coherent music that each one acting alone could not produce" (p. 197). Perhaps when it comes to AT one of our most challenging difficulties is that the very origin of AT was articulated in terms that has and sometimes still does address acting as a single-agent activity. The legacy of titles like *An actor prepares,* or *Building a character* might have been entirely different if those titles had been "*Actors prepare*" or "*Building characters*".

Edelman's reference to jazz improvisation brings us back to Hoffman's work with robots, which has recently focused on improving audience reception of robots improvising with jazz musicians. In that work, he describes the importance of focusing the robot's attention on the human musician, and points out that the first theorist of a relocated space of an actor's focus was Sanford Meisner, whose work at some points encouraged the actor to focus much more on what Viewpoints would call "letting information come to you". The point of this relocation of focus is what drives work in multi-agent system design and its advantages are well articulated by Eberhart and Kennedy (2011), looking beyond single-agent theories in AI:

> Real social interaction is exchange but also something else, perhaps more important: individual exchange rules, tips and beliefs about how to process the information. Thus a social interaction typically results in a change in the thinking processes – not just the contents – of the participants. (pp. xiv–v)

In his article on musical improvisation involving a robot (2011), Guy Hoffman proposes that "musical performance is as much about visual choreography and visual communication as it is about tonal musical generation" (p. 20), which makes clear the way in which creating a robot that can convince an audience of its "proto-human" abilities requires programming that is highly interactive. Hoffman's work with the marimba-playing robot focuses heavily on anticipation in order to create "real-time musical coordination" (which echoes the actor's desire to work "in the moment"). He found that by locating much of the robot's attention onto visual communication between the robot and the human player, the audience "rate the robot as playing better, more like a human, as more responsive and as more inspired by the human" (p. 20).

Conclusion

In philosophical terms, for actors and robots, it feels as if we have travelled some distance now from either our linear or our circular S-T-A models – both of which suggest that the sensing, thinking and acting are all located within a single agent. Effective performance it seems, both for robots and for humans, is located/generated somewhere in the intersubjective space between robot:human and actor:ensemble. The idea of the intersubjective space in practice between actors is a particularly intriguing one. Perhaps what Viewpoints practitioners are suggesting is something more profound than an actor representing (and therefore comprehending) the mental state of a performing partner; perhaps their ideas are closer to an "enactive intersubjectivity" (Fuchs & DeJaegher, 2009), wherein the process itself generates common meaning:

> According to our concept, social understanding is primarily based on intercorporality; it emerges from the interactive practice and coordination of the persons involved. We do not need to form internal models or representations of others in order to understand and communicate with them. Social cognition rather develops as a practical sense, a musicality for . . . rhythms and patterns . . . (p. 485)

This idea leads us in turn to some of the tougher questions surrounding multi-agent systems and suggests that in querying the location of generative thought we are naturally raising some difficult ontological questions. This is an area of much growth and study currently, well outlined in Petrov and Scarfe (2015), which addresses dynamic aspects of being and also "the process-relational character of being itself" (p. viii). While these deeper ontological questions are beyond the scope of this essay, it seems appropriate to raise the development of work in this area, and to suggest that if there are similarities in ontological considerations that apply both to human and robot multi-agent systems, there are also many differences. Seibt (2016) rejects entirely the "temptingly easy strategy of treating HRI as fictionalist analogues to human-human interactions", and suggests that what is required where human:robot interaction is concerned is "an entirely new 'classificatory framework' for simulated social interactions" (p. 5).

I began this article looking at Guy Hoffman's assertion that AI could learn from AT, but I hope that a brief look at similarities in both areas will lead us to an inverted and balancing assertion: that AT has much to learn from AI, and I would suggest that such learning can only come about through a continued interdisciplinary dialogue and exchange about how human behaviour is structured as part of a dynamic social environment and how various approaches to simulated models work within specific contexts. This in turn would require that acting theorists and practitioners enter the debate in more rigorous terms regarding the kinds of epistemological and ontological questions we raise in our practice.

If my look at the similarities in the developmental trajectories of AT/practice and AI is in danger of falling into the "temptingly easy" danger Seibt describes, I hope that it does at least raise some interesting questions for both areas. While much of the earlier works of AT writers has centred in one way or the other on a kind of "inner programming", newer writing in the area seems to concern itself heavily with the kind of knowledge for actors that emerges without the "inner" or central control. And if the ontological differences are acknowledged, it is still safe to say that the aims of the HRI wing of AI – as developed by Guy Hoffman and others – are closely aligned to those of the acting community: to create embodied, enactive experiences that convince and engage their audiences completely.

Notes

1. I employ the term 'acting theory (AT)' here in the way that Hoffman does – in relation to acting practitioners who have written about their practical methodology of training/directing actors.
2. I use 'parasitic' here as a simple metaphor for the character/actor relationship, and not in reference to 'parasitic speech acts' or specific language 'performativity'.
3. Most recently, John Lutterbie speaks of Stanislavski's early works as not addressing the body, "other than to acknowledge that the work of the actor must be given a form in order to be communicated to the spectator, which work requires bodily techniques. Beyond this acknowledgment, Stanislavski understands the body to contain the work done by the actor." He goes on to describe the change in Stanslavski's writings, in which he "rethought the role" of the body entirely. 31–32.
4. The difficulties of course with 'SENSE → THINK → ACT' models lie in the very linearity that is described in the model, and many contemporary researchers in AI are pursuing, amongst other things, 'loosely coupled' or, 'parallel processing' systems which attempt to solve the limitations of linear models with more connectivist, networked or parallel models. These things are beyond my work here, but we must recognise that for all its ease of description, there are, of course, problems with any simple, linear model of cognition.
5. The references to Viewpoints throughout this article refer specifically to *The viewpoints book* by Bogart and Landau (2005), and not to workshop participation.
6. References to Suzuki's training refer specifically to his book, *The Way of Acting*, and not to workshop participation.

Disclosure statement

No potential conflict of interest was reported by the author.

References

Aloimonos, Y. (Ed.). (1993). *Active perception*. Hillsdale, NJ: Lawrence Erlbaum Associates.

Bogart, A., & Landau, T. (2005). *The viewpoints book*. New York, NY: Theatre Communications Group.

Brighton, H., & Selina, H. (2003). *Artificial intelligence: A graphic guide*. London: Icon Publishing.

Brooks, R. A. (1991). Intelligence without representation. *Artificial Intelligence, 47*(1–3), 139–159. doi:10.1.1.12.1680

Chemero, A. (2011). *Radical embodied cognitive science*. Cambridge, MA: MIT Press.

Clark, A. (1998). *Being there (putting brain, body and world together)*. Cambridge, MA: MIT Press.

Dennett, D. (1993). *Consciousness explained*. London: Little, Brown.

Eberhart, R. E., & Kennedy, J. (2011). *Swarm intelligence*. San Francisco, CA: Morgan Kaufman Publishing.

Edelman, G. M. (1989). *The remembered present: A biological theory of consciousness*. New York: Basic Books.

Fuchs, T., & DeJaegher, H. (2009). Enactive intersubjectivity: Participatory sense-making and mutual incorporation. *Phenomenology and the Cognitive Sciences, 8*(4), 465–486. doi:10.1007/s11097-009-9136-4

Hoffman, G. (2011). *On stage: Robots as performers*. Unpublished paper. Retrieved from http://guyhoffman.com/publications/HoffmanRSS11Workshop.pdf

Hoffman, G. (2012). Embodied cognition for autonomous interactive robots. *Topics in Cognitive Science, 4*(4), 759–772. doi:10.1111/j.1756-8765.2012.01218.x. http://guyhoffman.com/publications/HoffmanTopiCS12.pdf

Hoffman, G., & Weinberg, G. (2011). Interactive improvisation with a robotic marimba player. In J. Solis & K. Ng (Eds.), *Musical robots and multimodal interactive multimodal systems*. Berlin: Springer Tracts in Advanced Robotics. Retrieved from http://guyhoffman.com/publications/HoffmanAuRo11.pdf

Kaag, J. (2008). The neurological dynamics of the imagination. *Phenomenology and Cognitive Neuroscience, 8*:2. Springer Press (Winter). doi:10.1.1.471.2279

Lutterbie, J. (2011). *Toward a general theory of acting: Cognitive science and performance*. New York, NY: Palgrave Macmillan.

Petrov, V., & Scarfe, A. C. (Eds.). (2015). *Dynamic being: Essays in process-relational ontology*. Newcastle-Upon-Tyne: Cambridge Scholars Publishing.

Pulvermüller, F. (2013). Semantic embodiment, disembodiment, or misembodiment? In search of meaning in modules and neuron circuits. *Brain and Language, 127*(1), 86–103. doi:10.1016/j.bandl.2013.05.015

Seibt, J. (2016). Draft unpublished article (in press), *Towards an ontology of simulated social interaction–varieties of the 'As If' for Robots and Humans*. Retrieved from http://www.academia.edu/19415782/Towards_an_Ontology_of_Simulated_Social_Interaction–Varieties_of_the_As_If_for_Robots_and_Humans

Soto-Morettini, D. (2010). *The philosophical actor*. Bristol: Intellect Books.

Suzuki, T. (1990). *The way of acting*. New York, NY: Theatre Communications Group.

Turing, A. M. (1950). Computing machinery and intelligence. *Mind, 49*, 433–460. Retrieved from http://phil415.pbworks.com/f/TuringComputing.pdf

An earned presence: studying the effect of multi-task improvisation systems on cognitive and learning capacity

Pil Hansen and Robert J. Oxoby

ABSTRACT

In this article, we articulate preliminary insights from two pilot studies. These studies contribute to an ongoing process of developing empirical, cross-disciplinary measures to understand the cognitive and learning effects of complex artistic practices – effects that we situate between theory of embodied concepts and conceptually calibrated physical attention and action. The stage of this process that we report on here was led by the cognitive performance studies scholar and dramaturge, Pil Hansen, and undertaken in collaboration with the experimental psychologist, Vina Goghari, and the behavioural economist, Robert Oxoby, assisted by four research assistants from Drama, Music, and Psychology at the University of Calgary. Our team set out to test the following hypothesis: *Active participation in performance generating systems has a positive effect on advanced student performers' working memory capacity, executive functions, and learning*. Our results have implications, in particular, for understandings of embodied learning in the educational sector, however a perhaps more significant contribution is a better understanding of the measures and constructs needed to arrive at a more complex, yet operational concept of embodied learning and forward the experimental study of relationships between performing arts practices, cognition, and learning.

Abductive inferences behind the hypothesis

Our experimental intervention, Performance Generating Systems, has been defined elsewhere by Hansen as a systematic and semi-closed form of improvisation in dance, theatre, and music: a dramaturgy of multiple, pre-identified tasks, rules of engagement, and source materials within the boundaries of which performers interact on stage (Hansen, 2015, pp. 124–125). Within a Performance Generating System, as opposed to more open forms of improvisation, performers must work attentively and simultaneously on multiple tasks while remaining aware of limiting rules. The source materials (such as movement sequences, memories of movement, or score text) are predefined and recycled by the performers while working on these tasks. These systems generate a performance on stage and in front of audiences where self-organising patterns of interaction arise over time, but are neither set nor necessarily repeatable.

Here, we report on and discuss two pilot studies that were specifically designed to empirically test interesting, but previously anecdotal observations made in other contexts. Within a past research project, *Acts of Memory*, Hansen conducted open, qualitative interviews with 14 dance and theatre performers from the Canadian companies (Theatre Replacement and Public Recordings) regarding their investment of autobiographical memory and trained memorisation skills in performance generating systems. The performers also discussed the specific aspects of the performance tasks they had experienced as easy or challenging. Without being asked directly, six performers independently commented on how these systems began to affect what they attended to, how they perceived both their actions and those of others, and when their general learning (within the system) made challenging tasks easier. In other words, they reported a cognitive effect, which could be caused by the specific praxis. Hansen has co-taught the systems to students whose ability to work analytically with complex concepts advanced beyond the level those same students were able to achieve in her other courses. In the open-ended comments section of course evaluations, students ascribed their learning achievements to experiences they had during practical, physical workshops. In addition to testing these anecdotal observations in our pilot studies, we also sought to explore whether there could be a connection between the cognitive effect reported by experienced performers and the learning effect reported by students.

As is typical for pilot studies, we turned towards well-established tools within our respective disciplines when selecting tests and data analysis methods to measure the cognitive and learning effects of our intervention: performance generating systems. That said, these measures reflect what we thought an effect might be related to and what we more specifically thought was affected. In short, we chose to utilise quantitative tests of working memory and fluid intelligence as measures, hypothesising that the cognitive needs of participating in a performance generating system may manifest in such measures. To study learning effects, we applied a combination of deductive and inductive qualitative coding categories. These were designed to reveal relationships between conceptual and physical learning engagement with reference to the notion of embodied learning while also identifying the primary factors that impacted these relationships over time. A more detailed introduction of these tools will be offered later. First we take a closer look at the demands our intervention may place on cognitive systems and how it can be understood through an embodied cognition framework.

In a performance generating system, the performers' work on complex tasks within restrictive rules that demand sustained activation of often competing foci of attention (see Hansen & House, 2015). In the example of the choreographer Ame Henderson and Public Recordings' "futuring memory" system, the dancers' meta-task was to work towards unison together and without surrendering the individual. Unison is a form of simultaneous dancing that normally depends on the perfect execution and timing of a choreographer's set and rehearsed choreography, effectively demanding that the dancer surrenders his or her individuality to become a seamless part of the group. In the futuring memory system, rules were established to ensure that dancers did not replace their conventional role in a unison formation with that of a leader or follower (e.g. dancers were not allowed to copy each other). A task called "futuring" was developed as a solution to the problem of how to work on unison without copying; dancers were tasked to form conscious hypotheses about where their co-dancers would go next, and then meet them there. Honouring the embodied memory and repertoire of choreography danced in the past, which dancers implicitly draw upon for improvised work, a task of "futuring memory" was added to the system. Dancers were invited to bring pre-identified sources (i.e. specific memories of past dances) into the work by recalling them when prompted by a physical association. The rest of the group would continue to future the recalling dancer and each other, while the recalling dancer had to recall transparently – that is, adapting to the physicalised hypotheses of the group rather than developing their own hypotheses of other's movement. When this performance generating system is engaged, the dancers have to sustain simultaneous attention to five competing foci:

(1) Perceiving the difference between the trajectory of one's own movement and that of everyone else's movement.
(2) Forming hypotheses about how the group will move in the moment after right now.
(3) Realising these hypotheses in movement, trying to meet the group where it is going next.
(4) Registering moments when a physical posture or movement aligns associatively with a set of past choreography, which can then be performed.
(5) Minding rules: leading, following, and copying are not allowed.

The challenge proposed by the system is largely impossible to meet; dancers try, sustain the attention for a while, start shifting, catch themselves copying, adjust and refocus, again and again. The effort involved is exhausting and the learning curve that sustained attention to these foci depends upon is steep and relentless. When dancers' skills improve and they get better at futuring each other's memories, new dancers, memory sources, or rules are introduced in order to keep the dancers' efforts alive and revitalise the system's ability to generate unpredictable performance (Hansen, 2015, pp. 129–130).

Our theoretical foundation and choice of measures are based on concepts from experimental, cognitive psychology that informed our understanding of these foci. Consider a "futuring dancer" who is attending to task execution while abiding by the rules of a given performance generating system. This dancer's perceptual orientation depends on using current information to form conscious hypotheses about where performers are going to meet in the next moment of the performance (i.e. the moment after right now). This orientation is kinaesthetic (i.e. cross-modal), including the performer's proprioception and motor system, peripheral visual perception, and auditory perception. At the same time, the direction of attention needed to train and presently sustain these modes of perception demands executive control within working memory. Although there are many theories of working memory, core to most models is the proposal that working memory involves the temporary storage and processing of information that is either perceived in the present or drawn from long-term memory. Such working memory processes include attending to and mentally manipulating information while suppressing distractions (Lawlor-Savage & Goghari, 2016; Miyake & Shah, 1999), both of which are involved in the task of futuring memory. The problem-solving involved in forming futuring hypotheses also depends on higher executive functions, applied with fluency and in flow. As performers learn their co-dancers' patterns of response, apply multiple foci of attention simultaneously, and shift between the futuring and recall tasks, they may train cognitive flexibility and generation

(Lövdén, Bäckman, Lindenberger, Schaefer, & Schmiedek, 2010). The rules (e.g. do not follow, lead, or copy) counter the learned skills and habits that are coded in the performers' implicit procedural and episodic long-term memory. Thus, the executive function of inhibition is added to our cognitive matrix. In other words, instead of primarily perceiving and responding through memory without conscious awareness (as is the norm), performance generating systems aim to inhibit long-term memory, expanding the performer's attention to sensory stimuli in the present and enhancing the performer's ability to process stimuli using executive function skills (e.g. working memory capacity, cognitive flexibility, and generation).

Within a framework more familiar to dance and performance studies, what likely is earned through the effort of performing this impossible multi-task is an enhanced performance presence that does not rely on "getting out of your head" but trains a mindful body and embodied mind. As Henderson expresses it, when performing in these systems "thinking is doing and doing is thinking" (Hansen, Kaeja, & Henderson, 2014, p. 30). As such, the practices of performance generating systems simultaneously require heightened executive control, motor awareness, sensory attention to co-performers, and analytical reflection on relations among performers, thereby pushing past the Cartesian body–mind dualism found in some dance, theatre, and performance studies frameworks. These frameworks include extremes such as forms of semiotic structuralism that regard physical action as a semiotic sign available for meaningful interpretation, constructivist approaches that dissolve the sensory capacity of the biological body into social constructions, and counter-responses that default to using a metaphysics of the body as a framework of study.

Embodiment and embodied learning capacity

Body–mind dualism is so engrained in social practices within and beyond dance and performance that direct attempts to apply theories of embodied cognition can come up against boundaries. There are ample and well-established theories of embodied cognition, action-based language, and concept-motor interactions with varying degrees of grounding in 4E philosophy and the cognitive sciences, including experimental psychology (e.g. Edelman & Tononi, 2000; Glenberg & Gallese, 2012; Noë, 2004; Rodriguez, McCabe, Nocera, Reilly, & Norbury, 2012; Thompson, 2007). These understandings have inspired artists, dance scientists, and cognitive performance scholars, giving rise to a growing research field (e.g. Hansen, 2016; Kemp, 2017; Lutterbie, 2011; Sofia, 2016). This work has found its way into higher education as theory of acting and performance reception, but, to our knowledge, the field has not yet advanced the same approach to enhance learning, nor tested the effects on learning of creative practices that challenge body–mind dualisms. Yet, a comparatively far more widespread application of embodied cognition is in the area of education and learning, where the frameworks closely match Piaget's influential theories from the 1950s. As demonstrated by Carly Kontra et al. in a current overview of embodied learning approaches, non-artistic pedagogical applications tend to place the body at the service of semantic and conceptual learning (Kontra, Goldin-Meadow, & Beilock, 2012, pp. 736–737). For example, physical movement is used to create simple bodily representations of mathematical terms and concepts to help students grasp math. While the enhanced learning effect of such embodied learning instruments is well documented (e.g. Broaders, Cook, Mitchell, & Goldin-Meadow, 2007; Goldin-Meadow, Cook, & Mitchell, 2009), the use of predominantly semantic and conceptual learning objectives makes these studies less relevant in the context of creative and emergent learning processes. An example of an inversed hierarchy from the field of dance, which presents comparable strengths and limitations, can be found in Martin Puttke's application of cognitive imaging and memorisation exercises when teaching advanced classical ballet. Using cognition as a tool to arrive at precise physical execution, Puttke places cognitive tasks at the service of codified physical learning objectives (2010, pp. 110–111).

The embodied learning potential Hansen finds relevant in the context of contemporary performing arts education lies in feedback effects between (i) embodied engagement with concepts and (ii) conceptual engagement with embodied experience. Here, the focus is on identifying the kinds of learning that produce conscious, enactive insight (self-reflexive learning capacity), instead of definitions or perfect execution (absorption of predefined knowledge). This form of self-reflexive learning is what we hypothesise that participation in performance generating systems will facilitate. It is possible that these systems reconcile body–mind dualism through tasks and rules of performance that simultaneously demand conscious intellectual control, heightened sensory-motor awareness, and attention to relational dynamics while "unlearning" trained habits and learning new cognitive practices.

When taking this step we would like to specify how we position our research in current discussions of embodied cognition. Several empirical theories exist regarding the close relationships between the motor and linguistic systems, ranging in arguments from all concepts are embodied (i.e. understood through or mapped onto physical experience; see Gallese & Lakoff, 2005; Glenberg, 2015; Glenberg & Gallese, 2012), to the perspective that either embodied language comprehension or the impact of language on movement depend on the extent to which concepts are motor action salient (e.g. Dove, 2011; Rodriguez et al., 2012; Sidhu, Heard, & Pexman, 2016). It is widely accepted that the motor system plays a role in perceiving action verbs and nouns that are closely associated with physical actions (see Pexman, 2017) and there is significant evidence that the production of such verbs can affect physical posture and movement (Rodriguez et al., 2012). However, to our knowledge, there is no empirical evidence for the embodiment of abstract concepts (see Dove, 2016; Pecher, Boot, & Van Dantzig, 2011; Zdrazilova & Pexman, 2013 for recent discussions of this problem). As Pexman indicates in her review paper on embodied conceptual development, empirical research finds greater support for emotional salience than motor salience in the development and comprehension of abstract concepts (Pexman, 2017, pp. 13–17). To us, these discussions indicate that the field of embodied cognition is maturing: the early phase of perhaps overgeneralised theories has now transitioned to a phase of asking critical questions, revising past research results, and experimentally examining ranges of embodiment.

It is not coincidental that we focus on two braches of otherwise distinct research into the relationship between motor and linguistic systems: cognitive linguistics and kinesiology. In the performing arts, the discovery that action-salient linguistic concepts affect body posture and movement is as relevant as the insight that motor memory (i.e. physical experience) affects the perception of action-salient concepts. This feedback effect and reciprocal reliance does reflect the practice of assigning concepts to physical actions within dance and theatre, both for purposes of memorisation and instant recall (Kemp, 2017) and in order to bring out certain qualities of expression. To a lesser extent, this feedback effect provides a framework for understanding the productivity of creative strategies and tasks that are simultaneously demanding attention to intellectual conceptualisation and heightened sensory-motor awareness (Hansen, 2016), as in performance generating systems. However, in order to arrive at self-reflexivity in creative learning processes, we need to consider more than action-salient concepts and their related motor actions, it becomes necessary to work with abstract concepts that allow a higher degree of generalisation of experience as well as complex, specialised movement approaches that are not reflected in action-salient concepts. For example, how can "presence" be experienced as conscious inhibition of trained movement skill and heightened sensory attention to the surroundings? In the performing arts, such an understanding of an abstract concept can neither be grasped through physical praxis nor conceptual analysis alone.

As it will be evident from our later discussion of learning capacity pilot results, participants reached an advanced understanding of the concept of presence through both the sensory-motor experience of, for example, falling into copying while "futuring" and the cognitive attempt to inhibit this trained response and instead redirect perceptual attention to the movement of others, possibly sustaining attention past normative working memory capacity. In turn, these physical, cognitive, and sensory experiences were reflected upon, understood, and advanced with reference to the concept of presence. The ability to generalise from sensory-motor experience to an abstract concept through more complex and less directly action-salient movement is exactly the embodied learning capacity that Hansen seeks to better understand and enhance in the the performing arts. In the context of performance generating systems, the cognitive demands of the performance tasks (operation of dual tasks, inhibition, cognitive flexibility, and working memory capacity), could be central to the engagement with and development of embodied learning capacity. It is possibly by meeting such demands that participants in our pilot studies became aware and able to relate abstract concepts to the cognitive challenges experienced while producing complex movement.

Two pilots

Our two pilots were designed around an intensive five-day course on performance generating systems with 20 advanced dance, theatre, and music students. Hansen taught this course with Valentina Bertolani (PhD Candidate in Music) and Christopher House (Artistic Director of Toronto Dance Theatre) in January 2016. Each of the first four days was dedicated to a collective investigation of how a specific system works (how it affects the performers and generates performance) with the fifth day dedicated to students creating their own systems.

The following systems were introduced as interventions (see original production images in Figure 1):

Day 1: Ame Henderson and Public Recording's "futuring memory" system from the dance work *relay* (2010);

Day 2: Paul Bettis's theatrical rule play *The Freud Project* (1996);

Day 3: Cornelius Cardew's Paragraph 7 from his music composition *The Great Learning* (1960s);

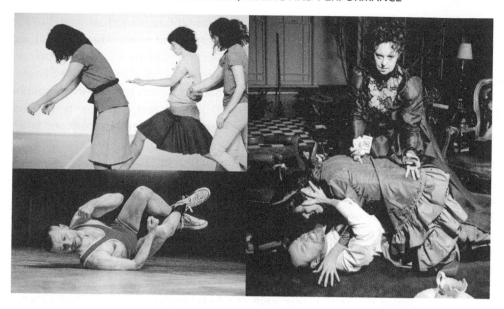

Figure 1. l-r: *Relay* 2010, photo by Ömer Yükseker; *I'll Crane for You* 2015, photo by Alejandro Santiago; *The Freud Project* 1996, photo by Paul Bettis.

Day 4: Christopher House's adaptation of Deborah Hay's solo dance score *I'll Crane for You* (2015).

For each system, we typically discussed the contextual practices of improvisation, notation, and artistic inquiry and identified specific system tasks, rules, and sources based on analysis of provided readings. Students then watched archival recordings of the systems while extracting observations for later exchange about the performers' perceptual orientation and attention, rules in action, and arising patterns. The second half of the day was dedicated to practical, physical workshops and performance of a system, with participants extracting observations for discussion of how the system affects the performers and generates performance. Students were tasked with posting a minimum of four daily observations drawn from their readings, group discussions, the contributions of other participants, or their experience of self and others in performance. They were instructed that the postings should engage with the overall inquiry of how the systems work. To develop this line of inquiry, a set of key concepts were introduced on the first day and returned to over the week. These concepts were "presence, reconstructive memory, perceptual attention, and awareness". On the fifth day students created their own systems and, in the weeks that followed, they submitted more developed written reflections on how their systems worked along with performance recipes. The latter is a both graphic and written presentation of the components of a system (source materials, tasks, rules, etc.) that generate performance along with instructions for how to engage them through rehearsal and performance. It is meant as an open source recipe, a method for sharing with other artists the generative architecture of these otherwise elusive creations across time and space.

Following a protocol approved by the Conjoint Faculties Research and Ethics Board, 13 of these students participated as research subjects and a comparable group were recruited as control subjects. Both groups had equal gender representation and balanced distribution of participants from the disciplines of dance, theatre, and music. The first pilot was designed to test the effect of the performance generating systems on working memory capacity and selected executive functions through cognitive measures. We used Engle's Automated Operation Span (AOS) test to measure working memory capacity in the context of a dual task (Unsworth, Heitz, Schrock, & Engle, 2005). In this test, participants were first asked to retain numbers, then they were presented with math problems to solve, and finally they were asked to recall their retained numbers in accurate order. This procedure was repeated with increasingly longer numbers until the participant reached his or her capacity limit and no longer could recall numbers while solving problems correctly. Delis–Kaplan Executive Function System (DKEFS) colour-word interference and design fluency tests were administered to measure executive inhibition and cognitive flexibility. The DKEFS design fluency also measured generation of designs, thought to index creativity (Delis, Kaplan, & Kramer, 2001). In the colour-word interference tests participants were presented with a test pad showing a variety of colour blocks within which the word of a different colour is written. In various test conditions the participant was asked to complete tasks like naming the colour, or naming the written text, each of which involves inhibiting their processing of irrelevant colour information. The design fluency test sheet displays squares with either filled or empty dots. The participants were asked to create novel designs tracing lines between dots under a series of different conditions, such as "use empty dots only" or "switch between filled and empty dots". These tests were completed before and after the intervention, alongside questionnaires collecting demographic information, motivation, and expectations of the types of changes this class would bring. More specifically, on an information questionnaire participants were asked to indicate the following variables: age; gender; cultural background(s); whether or not they had a cognitive health condition; the amounts of course credits completed in respectively dance, drama, and music; amount of courses taken involving improvisation; years of training in these disciplines; and years of improvisation practice. On pre- and post-motivation questionnaires administered before and after the intervention, participants were asked to indicate on a scale from 1–7 (1 being the lowest, 4 average or neither/nor, and 6 being the highest or significant) how motivated they were to take the course prior to the first day and and how motivated they where while taking the course; how much new insight and skill they expected to take away and did take away from the course; how challenging they expected to find or did find the course; whether any challenges experienced might become easier or did become easier over time; and whether their "way of experiencing (incl. perceiving, thinking, doing)" would change or did change over the course? The control group was tested at the same time interval, but without participating in any of the performance interventions and, of course, without filling in the pre- and post-questionnaires. These tests produced numeric performance scores that, given the small sample size, were analysed statistically using non-parametric texts (Wilcoxon rank-sum tests).

The second pilot looked into learning capacity and embodiment. The 13 participants' daily observations, their final written reflections, and video recordings from class were coded by two research assistants in the qualitative research software NVivo. The assistants used two kinds of codes: (1) pre-established codes that were derived from our hypothetical inferences and examined the inferences deductively and (2) new grounded codes that were inductively generated from the data, allowing for the discovery of novel factors and relationships. Among the pre-established codes were learning categories, which research assistants used to identify participant observations that were engaging with respectively semantic, practical, conceptual, or experiential knowledge. To relate developments in participant engagement across these categories to both the practical workshops and the analytical discussions of each course day, we also chose codes of "how the system works", "system properties" (tasks, rules, sources), and a series of abstract key concepts (presence, perceptual attention, memory, and awareness) of relevance to the systems. More specifically, the video recordings and text that form our qualitative data were uploaded as sources to Nvivo and the pre-determined codes were established in the software. Initially working together, and later working individually but reconvening regularly to test and align their coding practices and interpretation of emerging codes, two of the research assistants went through these sources one by one marking utterances that matched one or several of the codes, linking them to the specific codes in the software. When new concerns, issues, or concepts emerged as potential factors to the research assistants they discussed them with the full group, arrived at conceptual clarity, and then implemented them as new codes working backwards through the data. Emerging subcategories were considered and implemented using the same procedure. The research assistants finished processing the daily observations and generated the following grounded codes: challenges, comparison to conventions, individual focus, and group orientation. When analysing the coded data, Hansen compared changes in the participants' engagement with the different types of knowledge to their comprehension of the key notions and their focus on the remaining subjects coded. The goal of this qualitative analysis was to uncover the relationships and patterns that most significantly affected the participants' learning process and achievements and then compare them to our hypothesis. Central to this analysis was thus the question of whether or not a relationship could be detected between attention to experiential, sensory-motor learning and advances in participants' ability to comprehend abstract concepts, as well as the identification of factors that affected such a relationship.

Preliminary results: quantitative measures

Overall, the result of the cognitive capacity tests are neutral: the group that took the course scored neither better nor worse on post-tests relative to pre-tests than the control group. Across all AOS and DKEFS tests we find no differences in either composites or the individual items (Wilcoxon $p > .30$ in all areas). Further, we did not identify any significant changes (pre-/post-test differences statistically different from zero) in composites or individual items within the treatment and control groups. While this result neither supports nor provide new insight in regards to out hypothesis, it is consistent with the argument since put forth by Redick (2015) that training interventions are unlikely to produce measurable changes in individual higher-order cognitive functioning.

However, in two specific areas we do observe statistically identifiable differences between pre- and post-test performance by participants across the treatment and control groups that can motivate further studies with longer interventions. Specifically, participants in the treatment group showed moderate improvements in design fluency relative to those in the control group (Wilcoxon $p = .015$). This difference was detected within the data from a test condition measuring cognitive flexibility (set-shifting ability) and non-verbal creativity (ability to develop novel designs). Thus we can reject the null hypothesis that changes from pre- to post-test in design fluency across the treatment and control group were drawn from the same distribution. This is suggestive of participation in the performance generating system interventions reducing the errors in design fluency tests by 2 points relative to the control group. Although it also is broadly consistent with our initial hypothesis that the simultaneity of various processing functions required by a performance generating system may affect cognitive processing in some dimension, further steps are needed to identify such changes. We furthermore identified a marginal improvement of processing speed and a reduction in errors in the colour-word testing in the treatment group relative to the control group. However, while this improvement is not statistically significant (Wilcoxon $p = .10$), it is illustrative of the manner in which engagement in a performance generating system aims to sustain focus and continuous cognitive processing while inhibiting certain responses. This result provides a motivation for further research considering how a longer (i.e. beyond five days) intervention in a performance generating system may affect standard measures of working memory.

In conclusion, it appears our implemented training in performance generating systems did not produce fundamental changes in objective measures of cognition. This could either be (1) because there is no effect (leading to the rejection of our hypothesis) or (2) because our pilot with its 13 participants and five full days of intervention was underpowered to produce an objectively measurable effect. This interpretation is supported both by Redick's findings and the fact that we were unable to analyse our data using matrixes of the surveyed variables (e.g. a matrix of years of improvisation practice, discipline, and motivation) to reveal more defined differences, should they exist, because such subdivision resulted in sample groups that were too small (i.e. three or less). We submit that our objective measures suggest a small effect that is insufficient to adequately identify the actual changes provided by performance generating systems. However, a larger sample is unlikely to address this problem alone. In a current discussion of working memory tests, Foroughi, Monfort, Paczynski, McKnight, and Greenwood (2016) and others, argue that cognitive capacity is heritable and fairly stable. In a study that administered a popular working memory training intervention after an either suggestive or non-suggestive training invitation, they were able to produce a placebo effect equating to a 5–10 point improvement on IQ tests. This leads them to question the reading of the typically small effects on intelligence measured in experiments involving working memory training interventions.

A third interpretation of the cognitive capacity pilot results, which we cautiously support, is thus that there may have been a cognitive effect which could be expressed with greater statistical significance in a larger study if, and only if, new test measures that are better equipped to measure the subtle changes related to our intervention are developped.

This interpretation is supported by a puzzling finding that is drawn from the motivation questionnaires. On a scale from 1–7 (1 being "not at all", 5 "somehwhat" and 7 "yes, significantly"), the average indication of whether the participants felt their way of experiencing had changed was 6 on their post questionnaires. This score was merely a 7.57% increase from the average on the pre questionnaries. Like the small changes measured in the cognitive tests, the participants could be reporting a placebo effect wherein participants qualitatively perceived a change because they felt they "should" benefit from their classes and training. However open comments that the participants added on their surveys in extension of this question indicated that the expectations marked on the pre-motivation questionnaire were in regards to acquiring new skills or learning about new practices (i.e.

expectations that match other types of BFA and MFA courses) while many of the post-test scores referred to experiences that were more closely reflecting perceptual and cognitive processes. For example, compare the following pre- and post-questionnaire comments:

> I think that having the use of 3 disciplines will change the way I interact with creative processes. As well, performance generating systems is a new idea to me so I will hopefully take something away form that which will change how I perceive things. (Participant #9, pre-motivation questionnaire)

> There was a moment while working with Christopher where I felt like I had almost unlocked the secret to utilizing the frantic way my brain operates. I tend to experience hyper focus on tasks and subjects but I get distracted easily and the focus changes to something else. During one excercise I was shifting focus so rapidly that it was almost to the point of focusing on all aspects of the exercise at once. (participant #9, post-motivation questionnaire)

Interpreting the quantitative survey in relation to the qualitative differences exemplified above, our results do indicate an important discrepancy between the objective measures and participant experiences that cannot be explained as a placebo effect alone. This discrepancy suggests that our objective test measures (AOS, DKEFS) were unable to identify the reported effect and that different test measures need to be designed. Thus our results suggest several directions for further research into the relationships between performance, cognition, and learning.

Preliminary results: qualitative measures

The qualitative results from the learning capacity pilot yielded clearer, interpretive results. However, as relationships between multiple factors are drawn into matrices for analysis, the overlap between observations coded becomes smaller. Such matrixes thus provide weaker qualification of our interpretations than relationships that are drawn between fewer codes. The clearest result is demonstrated in the observations regarding the four knowledge and learning categories over the five days of the course. Participants started with a predominant focus on semantic and practical knowledge and ended with a significantly increased focus on experiential knowledge. This is in spite of the fact that the course facilitation was designed to equally teach all four categories every day. As indicated in the chart below, engagement with semantic knowledge and attempts to arrive at definitions decreased by 100%, engagement with practical knowledge of how to execute tasks decreased by 50%, and engagement with experiential knowledge increased by 50% (Figure 2).

Only the conceptual knowledge category remained consistent throughout the week, indicating a relationship between experiential and conceptual advancement. We did find a larger engagement of key concepts that are associated with experiential knowledge (awareness and perceptual attention) than the ones that initially were understood by participants as being theoretical and thus more abstract (memory and presence).

Furthermore, the participants achieving the most advanced understanding of these key concepts and how the systems work were all among the individuals who contributed the most experiential observations. However, the inverse is not true: one participant who posted a very high number of experiential observations did not advance much analytically. This individual stood out in two ways: the advancing participants sustained engagement with conceptual knowledge throughout the week and they transitioned from a focus on the

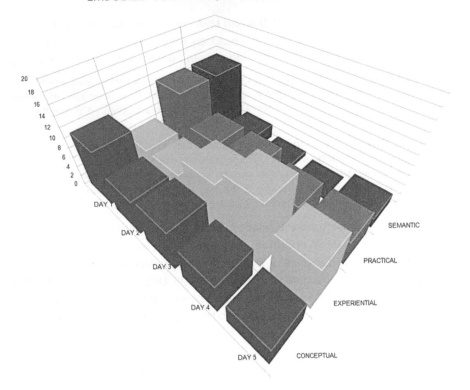

Figure 2. Matrix coding query – Results preview.

individual to a group focus within the first 2–3 days; the individual did neither. The only participant who neither increased her experiential nor conceptual observations but advanced significantly in the practical category was unable to participate physically and had to mostly observe after the second day. This suggests that increased engagement with experiential knowledge does depend on fully embodied practice and it provides further support for the conclusion that experiential and conceptual advancements are closely connected.

The participants posted more observations on "challenges" than on any other code subject. Initially these observations were practical and conceptual in focus, included negative comparisons to prior knowledge, and intersected with discussions of system *tasks*. Over the week, observations about challenges became practical and experiential in focus and shifted to primarily intersect with discussions of system *rules* and of how the systems work. In other words, the participants' early attempts to understand "what" a performance generating task is came up against a boundary of prior knowledge in practical and conceptual terms. The task did not match the foundation ideas of practice that participants were familiar with, and they were troubled by the need to step outside of their field of competence. Further into the course, they reflected on challenges experienced while attempting to remain aware of rules during task execution. Instead of comparing the experience to prior knowledge, they turned to discussions of habits, momentary loss of concentration, exhaustion, and difficulty distinguishing between different ways of attending, as they related to their growing understanding of how the system works and affects them. This was also the point at which participants began to associate their experience from within the sensory-motor praxis with the concepts that initially were considered the most abstract and theoretical.

> I found today's system extremely challenging. It wasn't so much that the required physicality was draining; rather, the level of concentration was. I was surprised at how "in my head" I had to be in order to keep track of all the points of attention I had to balance. . . . There were many points today throughout the exercise where my concentration slipped. . . . It would always take me a few seconds to register what was going on and then figure out how to solve the problem. (Participant # 6, observations posted on teaching portal, day 4)

This example was coded at "experiential" engagement with knowledge and the concept of "presence" and speaks to the challenge of concentration and attention that sustained performance presence requires while working physically in Deborah Hay and Christopher House's praxis. This praxis requires that the dancer responds to information from the surroundings and the body without planning or building sequences and without holding on to the information. In practical terms, the participants were trained and asked to continuously "turn their head" (i.e. shift point of visual and proprioceptive attention) in order to respond to new information while working on their interpretation of a written dance score.

> For the section when we were looking at the audience, we needed to have contact with the audience but not a connection with them. You need to be present in the moment to be able to differentiate between those two ideas. (Participant # 10, observations posted on teaching portal, day 4)

The example above is an observation on "presence" that was coded at both "experiential" and "conceptual", reflecting emerging overlap between these two forms of engagement. The following example was coded as a "conceptual" engagement with the concept of "memory". However at this stage of the course, knowledge that derives from the sensory-motor experience of working through challenges in practice informs the participant's conceptual reflection.

> The idea of surrendering myself to the system by unlearning what I knew and was comfortable with. Not to hold on to a moment, experience or idea, to get away from old habits, to disengage from what is not needed in the moment . . . These are all parameters that combined bring me to a place of intense vulnerability. It is extremely scary to go there. It is unknown and therefore, frightening. Without a probable ending nor possibility of achieving a goal. (Participant # 8, observations posted on teaching portal, day 4)

As mentioned, the literature on embodied learning describes the employment of movement in the service of semantic and conceptual understanding. If the movement-based and conceptual learning categories run parallel to each other in such a hierarchical relationship there should be no increase or decrease in engagement with either over time. In our pilot, participants' engagement with learning categories did change over time while they were actively "unlearning" prior knowledge as individuals and reflecting upon the challenges experienced around learning new cognitive practices as a group. Discrepancies between prior learning and the task at hand demanded conscious attention, so did moments when a rule became difficult to implement because of habits. It was partly through the participants' work on these barriers that they heightened their cognitive ability to remain attentive, inhibit, and multi-task while reporting on how the activity affected them as performers; and it is within this enhanced self-reflexivity that the key concepts gained operational meaning. In terms of embodied learning, the performance generating systems helped participants push past a hierarchical relationship between conceptual and experiential learning and instead establish a reciprocal relationship between the embodied understanding of concepts and conceptual engagement with movement. As previously discussed, empirical studies of embodiment in both cognitive linguistics and kinesiology are limited to measuring the embodiment effect of highly motor action-salient concepts. It is likely that the reciprocal relationship described above was instrumental for our participants' ability to achieve understandings of abstract concepts that were advanced through and embedded in self-reflexive experiences of complex sensory-motor praxis.

We are tempted to describe the learning principles discovered in this pilot as a form of fully embodied critical reflection. By taking on the challenge of performing a different cognitive practice, the participants became empowered to reflect upon and push beyond otherwise implicit past learning that informs their embodied conceptualisation of and responses to artistic tasks. In doing so they moved beyond physical engagement of action-salient concepts and began to develop new and more conceptually abstract phenomenological knowledge.

Recommendations: measures and transferability

What are the implications of the quantitative and qualitative findings of engagement with performance generating systems for measures of cognition? In reflection, performance generating praxis may be too complex to produce an objectively measurable effect on individual cognitive skills (cognitive flexibility, working memory capacity, etc.). Thus, while we do observe marginal changes in some cognitive performance skills (as measured by the DKEFS tests), a larger and more relevant effect might be on the *integration* of such skills, including modalities from both bottom-up and top-down cognition, kinaesthetic perception and conscious choice-making (i.e. embodied cognition). In other words, participants may have perceived changes at a more global level, rendering the cognitive tasks we introduced as test measures less relevant to the changes they experienced. Alternatively, it could be that the changes experienced after the performance generating systems class do not improve specific cognitive abilities, even though they are relevant to gestalt processing. Finally, it may be that the types of cognitive abilities that are affected in a performance generating system are not adequately identifiable given the measures we used, or even the set of existing measures in the field. Our pilots are illustrative of the type of study that crosses boundaries between embodied cognition, existing cognitive abilities, learning, and performance. The mere nature of performance generating systems may require alternate measures for the identification of the relationships between cognition and performance.

Generalisation from one form of learning to another form of learning has always been difficult to produce in cognitive science studies that apply far less complex learning interventions than Performance Generating Systems (Green & Bavelier, 2008; Melby-Lervåg & Hulme, 2013). Because of introducing more complex interventions, this challenge has become larger and is, effectively, forcing us to look for unconventional solutions. We are not alone in arriving at this conclusion in response to research processes that cross the performing arts and cognitive science (e.g. Hansen, 2017; Hansen & Barton, 2009, pp. 130–135; Jola, 2010, p. 211; Stevens, 2005, pp. 167–168), but while the solutions proposed and advanced by the field have produced methods for testing audience responses, understanding cognitive processes involved in expert performance, and setting up feedback loops between experimental research and creative practice, they do not, to our knowledge, attempt to measure transferable cognitive effects of performance practice and training. New solutions are needed to advance the embodied, cognitive psychology of learning into complex, intersubjective, and creative contexts.

How do we move forward? Our cognitive capacity pilot was measuring effects on transfer of performance generating skills to specific higher-level cognitive tasks. In the cognitive science literature, training studies often refer to three types of transfer: target, near, and far. Target transfer refers to improvement in the specific skills or tasks practiced. Near transfer refers to improvement in skills similar (i.e. in the same domain) to the ones trained (Morrison & Chein, 2011). For example, if we trained working memory, we would expect improvement on other working memory tasks that were not trained. Far transfer refers to improvement in skills that are in a different domain than those trained. For example, if we trained working memory, we would expect improvement in cognitive flexibility. In cognitive science, literature of most significance is typically demonstrating far transfer – the generalisability of training specific skills. In our qualitative pilot, we saw improvement in the specific skills practiced by the class from the first session to the last session, demonstrating *targeted* transfer. We only looked at the effect on academic performance within the intervention itself. Our quantitative cognitive pilot focused on *far* transfer. It measured whether the intervention had an effect on individual cognitive modalities when performing very different dual tasks. Perhaps in a new area that was a too ambitious choice. A focus on demonstrating near transfer would be beneficial, as far transfer without documented near transfer is difficult to interpret. It would also help us bypass the previously mentioned issues regarding far transfer readings of the effect of working memory training on higher cognitive functions that Foroughi et al. (2016) bring up. To arrive at more suitable, interdisciplinary ways of studying the cognitive and learning effects of performance generation, we propose the measurement and development of *near* transfer tests of *integrated* cognitive skills that match the relationships between learning categories and the reciprocal processes discovered in the learning capacity pilot. Such a test could include observation of the participants' skill integration when engaged in a complex, embodied multi-task, like a simulation of left side driving or an unfamiliar performance generating system. Further, methodological suggestions for such studies include larger sample sizes in order to allow for the investigation of factors that affect training outcomes (e.g. age, gender, training), and a better understanding of the relationship between subjective cognitive changes experienced and more objective cognitive tests.

Moreover, it is worth exploring whether engagement with a performance generating system has longer-term effects on both cognitive skills and embodied critical reflection. Our intervention focused on a one-week experience using differences in pre- and post-tests as measures of cognitive change and coding of participant observations as measures of embodied learning. Indeed, participation and use of performance generating systems may fundamentally change an individual's artistic practice. As this practice changes, it is likely that the cognitive skills and learning modalities employed will change and that the individual's embodied critical agency and practice will evolve. As such, this suggests approaching the relationship between cognitive skills, learning categories, and the use of performance generating systems as they form a longer arc over a performance practice.

Disclosure statement

No potential conflict of interest was reported by the author(s).

Funding

This work was supported by Social Sciences and Humanities Research Council of Canada [Enhancement Grant].

References

Broaders, S. C., Cook, S. W., Mitchell, Z., & Goldin-Meadow, S. (2007). Making children gesture brings out implicit knowledge and leads to learning. *Journal of Experimental Psychology: General, 136,* 539–550. doi:10.1037/0096-3445.136.4.539

Delis, D. C., Kaplan, E., & Kramer, J. H. (2001). *Dellis-Kaplan executive function system (D-KEFS).* San Antonio, TX: The Psychological Corporation.

Dove, G. (2011). On the need for embodied and dis-embodied cognition. *Frontiers in Psychology.* doi:10.3389/fpsyg.2010.00242

Dove, G. (2016). Three symbol ungrounding problems: Abstract concepts and the future of embodied cognition. *Psychonomic Bulletin & Review, 23*(4), 1109–1121. doi:10.3758/s13423-015-0825-4.

Edelman, G., & Tononi, G. (2000). *A universe of consciousness.* New York, NY: Basic Books.

Foroughi, C. K., Monfort, S. S., Paczynski, M., McKnight, P. E., & Greenwood, P. M. (2016). Placebo effects in cognitive training. *Procceedings of the National Academy Sciences, 113,* 7470–7474. doi:10.1073/pnas.1601243113

Gallese, V., & Lakoff, G. (2005). The brain's concepts: The role of the sensory-motor system in conceptual knowledge. *Cognitive Neuropsychology, 22,* 455–479.

Glenberg, A. M. (2015). Few believe the world is flat: How embodiment is changing the scientific understanding of cognition. *Canadian Journal of Experimental Psychology, 69,* 165–171.

Glenberg, A. M., & Gallese, V. (2012). Action-based language: A theory of language acquisition, comprehension, and production. *Cortex, 48,* 905–922. doi:10.1016/j.cortex.2011.04.010

Goldin-Meadow, S., Cook, S. W., & Mitchell, Z. A. (2009). Gesturing gives children New ideas about math. *Psychological Science, 5,* 664–674. doi:10.1111/j.1467-9280.2009.02297.x

Green, C. S., & Bavelier, D. (2008). Exercising your brain: A review of human brain plasticity and training-induced learning. *Psychol Aging, 23,* 692–701. doi:10.1037/a0014345

Hansen, P. (2015). The dramaturgy of performance generating systems. In P. Hansen & D. Callison (Eds.), *Dance dramaturgy: Modes of agency, awareness and engagement* (pp. 124–142). Basingstoke: Palgrave.

Hansen, P. (2016). The adaptability of language-motor connections in dance and acting: A coordination dynamics experiment. *MAPA D2, 3,* 5–15.

Hansen, P. (2017). Research-Based practice: Facilitating transfer across artistic, scholarly, and scientific inquiries. In A. Arlander, B. Barton, M. Dreyer-Lude, & B. Spatz (Eds.), *Performance as research: Knowledge, methods, impact.* forthcoming. London: Routledge.

Hansen, P., & Barton, B. (2009). Research-Based practice: Situating vertical city between artistic development and applied cognitive science. *TDR: The Drama Review, 53,* 120–136. doi:10.1162/dram.2009.53.4.120

Hansen, P., with House, C. (2015). Scoring the generating principles of performance systems. *Performance Research on An/Notation, 20,* 65–73. doi:doi:10.1080/13528165.2015.1111054

Hansen, P., Kaeja, K., & Henderson, A. (2014). Self-organization and transition in systems of dance generation. *Performance Research on Turbulence, 19,* 23–33.

Jola, C. (2010). Research and choreography: Merging dance and cognitive neuroscience. In B. Blaesing, M. Puttke, & T. Schack (Eds.), *The neurocognition of dance: Mind, motion and motor skill* (pp. 201–234). Hove: Psychology Press.

Kemp, R. (2017). Action, memory, and meaning: Embodied cognition and the fictional present. In P. Hansen & B. Bläsing (Eds.), *Performing the remembered present: The cognition of memory in dance, theatre, and music.* forthcoming. London: Methuen Bloomsbury.

Kontra, C., Goldin-Meadow, S., & Beilock, S. L. (2012). Embodied learning across the life span. *Topics in Cognitive Science, 4,* 731–739. doi:10.1111/j.1756-8765.2012.01221.x

Lawlor-Savage, L., & Goghari, V. M. (2016). Dual N-back working memory training in healthy adults: A randomized comparison to processing speed training. *PLoS ONE, 11*, e0151817. doi:10.1371/journal.pone.0151817

Lövdén, M., Bäckman, L., Lindenberger, U., Schaefer, S., & Schmiedek, F. (2010). A theoretical framework for the study of adult cognitive plasticity. *Psychological Bulletin, 136*, 659. doi:10.1037/a0020080

Lutterbie, J. (2011). *Towards a theory of acting: Cognitive science and performance*. Basingstoke: Palgrave.

Melby-Lervåg, M., & Hulme, C. (2013). Is working memory training effective? A meta-analytic review. *Developmental Psychology, 49*, 270–291. doi:10.1037/a0028228

Miyake, A., & Shah, P. (1999). Toward unified theories of working memory: Emerging general consensus, unresolved theoretical issues, and future research directions. In A. Miyake & P. Shah (Eds.), *Models of working memory: Mechanisms of active maintenance and executive control* (pp. 442–481). Cambridge: Cambridge University Press.

Morrison, A. B., & Chein, J. M. (2011). Does working memory training work? The promise and challenges of enhancing cognition by training working memory. *Psychonomic Bulletin & Review, 18*, 46–60. doi:10.3758/s13423-010-0034-0

Noë, A. (2004). *Action in perception*. Cambridge, MA: MIT Press.

Pecher, D., Boot, I., & Van Dantzig, S. (2011). Abstract concepts: Sensory-motor grounding, metaphors, and beyond. *Psychology of Learning and Motivation, 54*, 217–248.

Pexman, P. M. (in press). The role of embodiment in conceptual development. *Language, Cognition and Neuroscience*.

Puttke, M. (2010). Learning to dance means learning to think! In B. Blaesing, M. Puttke, & T. Schack (Eds.), *The neurocognition of dance: Mind, motion and motor skills* (pp. 101–114). Hove: Psychology Press.

Redick, T. S. (2015). Working memory training and interpreting interactions in intelligence interventions. *Intelligence, 50*, 14–20. doi:10.1016/j.intell.2015.01.014

Rodriguez, A. D., McCabe, M. L., Nocera, J. R. Reilly, J., & Norbury, C. (2012). Concurrent word generation and motor performance: Further evidence for language-motor interaction. *PLoS ONE, 7*, e37094. doi:10.1371/journal.pone.0037094

Sidhu, D. M., Heard, A., & Pexman, P. M. (2016). Is more always better for verbs? Semantic richness effects and verb meaning. *Frontiers in Psychology, 7*, 798. doi:10.3389/fpsyg.2016.00798

Sofia, G. (2016). Introduction: Towards and embodied theatrology? In C. Falletti, G. Sofia, & V. Jacono (Eds.), *Theatre and cognitive neuroscience* (pp. 49–60). London: Bloomsbury Methuen.

Stevens, C. (2005). Trans-disciplinary approaches to research into creation, performance, and appreciation of contemporary dance. In R. Grove, C. Stevens, & S. McKechnie (Eds.), *Thinking in four dimensions* (pp. 154–168). Melbourne: Melbourne University Press.

Thompson, E. (2007). *Mind in life: Biology, phenomenology, and the sciences of mind*. Cambridge, MA: Harvard University Press.

Unsworth, N., Heitz, R. P., Schrock, J. C., & Engle, R. W. (2005). An automated version of the operation span task. *Behavior Research Methods, 37*, 498–505. doi:10.3758/BF03192720

Zdrazilova, L., & Pexman, P. M. (2013). Grasping the invisible: Semantic processing of abstract words. *Psychonomic Bulletin & Review, 20*, 1312–1318.

The embodied performance pedagogy of Jacques Lecoq

Rick Kemp

ABSTRACT

This article proposes that acting is a valuable area of research for the fields of Artificial Intelligence and Simulated Behaviour. This suggestion is supported through applying theories and findings from the field of embodied cognition to the performance pedagogy of French acting teacher Jacques Lecoq (1921–1999). Embodied cognition proposes that thinking and behaviour are properties of the whole human organism, not the brain alone, and that body, brain and cognition are "situated" – engaged with the surrounding environment. This thesis arises from findings that show that sensorial and motor experiences form the neural foundations for mental concepts and that sensorimotor neural networks are partially re-activated by mental and linguistic activity, leading to the concept of "embodied simulation". I give examples of the ways in which Lecoq's conceptualisation of acting technique is implicitly congruent with the principles of embodied cognition, and often explicitly anticipates its precepts.

Introduction

Acting technique is a valuable area of research for the fields of Artificial Intelligence and Simulated Behaviour. In many senses, acting is Simulated Behaviour. Actors preparing and playing a role engage in most, if not all, of the cognitive processes that humans conduct in daily life – with a crucial difference. Actors consciously elicit and regulate phenomena that generally arise spontaneously for most people. These phenomena include imagination, memory, empathy, emotion stimulation and regulation, interpersonal awareness, and narrative, linguistic, and psychological analysis among many other activities. It is these cognitive activities, in addition to the more easily recognised aspects of speech, voice, facial expression, gesture and movement, that comprise an actor's technique. The visibility of technique varies according to style and medium. In the hyper-naturalism of most Western screen drama actors strive to appear to respond spontaneously to events, creating an apparent naturalness of behaviour in fictional circumstances. In fact, this naturalness is generally the result of many years of training and long and painstaking preparation for individual roles. An understanding of the ways in which actors formulate and practice technique can offer researchers in the field of Artificial Intelligence valuable insights into the conscious eliciting of otherwise unconscious behaviour.

In Western theatre, actor training as a dedicated activity arose predominantly in the twentieth century, with varied forms of apprentice systems largely responsible for the development of technique prior to this. The most influential formulator of contemporary acting technique in the west was Russian actor and director Konstantin Stanislavski (1863–1938), who developed a system for preparing a role that is widely taught in European and Western influenced theatre conservatoires. His work is analysed from a cognitive perspective elsewhere in this issue. Stanislavski's approach is largely applied to text-based performance and associated mainly with the style of psychological realism that has been prevalent on stage and screen in the second half of the twentieth century and early part of this century. By contrast, the performance pedagogy of Jacques Lecoq (1921–1999) deals mainly with improvisation, deliberately avoids language in its early stages, engages with multiple styles of performance and explicitly seeks to stimulate the creation of new forms of performance. It is a training system for actors that is radically different from Stanislavski's, yet the two are widely used alongside one another in Western actor training programmes, suggesting that in practice they complement each other. In this article I propose that Lecoq's conceptualisation of acting technique is implicitly congruent with the principles of embodied cognition, and often explicitly forecasts its precepts. When viewed in the theoretical framework of embodied cognition, many of Lecoq's training practices consciously elicit and define what would otherwise be unconscious activity, articulating techniques that demonstrate the dynamic and constructive nature of meaning as broadly posited in the concept of embodied simulation. I will give a brief overview of some of the relevant principles of embodied cognition and then relate these to aspects of Lecoq's pedagogy giving some specific examples.

Embodied cognition

Embodied cognition proposes that thinking and behaviour are properties of the whole human organism, not the brain alone, and that body, brain and cognition are "situated" – engaged with the surrounding environment. This presents a radical challenge to the Cartesian separation of mind from body that has long influenced traditional Western psychology. The field of embodied cognition incorporates research from many related disciplines – psychology, linguistics and neurobiology among many others – and inevitably contains varied opinions. Certain concepts, however, are considered foundational. One of these is the principle that has emerged from neuroscientific findings that sensorial and motor experiences form the neural foundations for mental concepts.

As cognitive linguist George Lakoff and cognitive philosopher Mark Johnson explain:

> Our abilities to move the way we do and to track the motion of other things give motion a major role in our conceptual system. The fact that we have muscles and use them to apply force in certain ways leads to the structure of our system of causal concepts. What is important is that the peculiar nature of our bodies shapes our very possibilities for conceptualization and categorization [. . .]. (Lakoff & Johnson, 1999, p. 19)

This insight is evoked in the title of cognitive philosopher Shaun Gallagher's book *How the Body Shapes the Mind* (2006) and informs many other works (e.g. Gallese & Lakoff, 2005; Haggard, Rossetti, & Kawato, 2007; Johnson, 1987, 1993; Lakoff & Johnson, 1999; Varela, Thompson, & Rosch, 1991). This concept challenges assumptions that underlie much of

Western thought, since it demonstrates that mental concepts are shaped by physical experience in the material environment and exploit many of the same neural pathways that are involved in physical action and sensorial experience. Based on this understanding, phenomena such as consciousness, empathy, intersubjectivity, affect and aesthetic responses "come from having a body with various sensorimotor capacities [that] are themselves embedded in a more encompassing biological, psychological and cultural context" (Varela et al., 1991, p. 173). Within the field of embodied cognition there is a growing consensus that meaning results inter-subjectively from our situated interactions with the world. Thus meaning can be quite personal, as it depends on our particular experiences in particular environments. By extension, meaning is also variable across cultures. This theory of meaning depends on the notion of embodied simulation – the experience of perception and action without their physical manifestation. According to the embodied simulation hypothesis, meaning does not arise from the deployment of abstract mental symbols but is constructed from the neural experiences triggered by various stimuli and is thus dynamic and constructive. I will describe other aspects of theory from embodied cognition later. For now, I would like to trace the links between these fundamental precepts of embodied cognition and Lecoq's dictum of "Tout bouge" ("everything moves", "all is movement") and his concept of "Le fonds poetique commun" (translated below).

Jacques Lecoq – Tout bouge

The influence of Jacques Lecoq on modern theatre is significant. He founded an international school of performance training in Paris in 1956 at which he taught until a few days before his death in 1999. The school continues to thrive under the direction of Pascale Lecoq, Lecoq's daughter, and has trained over 5000 students from at least 84 countries. Many of these students have formed their own companies, such as Le Théâtre du Soleil in Paris, Complicite in London, Mummenschantz in Switzerland, Footsbarn in France and Pig Iron in Philadelphia as well as many others worldwide. Graduates have also found success as directors of theatre and film (e.g. Julie Taymor, Luc Bondy, Simon McBurney, James McDonald), or as actors in mainstream movies (e.g. Geoffrey Rush, Toby Jones and Sergi Lopez). Many others teach in actor training programmes or have founded their own schools in countries ranging from Chile to Germany to the USA to Belgium, Italy and Spain (for more information on Lecoq and his school see Evans & Kemp, 2016; Kemp, 2012; Lecoq, 2001, 2006; Murray, 2003). Lecoq's guiding principle was "Tout bouge" – everything moves. His rigourous analysis of movement in humans and their environments formed the foundation for a refined and nuanced repertoire of physical exercises. These develop a heightened somatic awareness in the actor of the relationship between thought, feeling, gesture and language, preparing him or her to communicate with movement in a variety of styles, to employ physical actions that both provoke and define emotion and to invest spoken language with meaningful gesture. Given the primacy that embodied cognition places on sensorimotor experience and its role in shaping meaning, Lecoq's focus on movement immediately resonates with its principles and the involvement of physical activity with communication. It must be remembered, however, that the ideas of embodied cognition are still in the process of gaining widespread recognition, and many people in mainstream theatre consider Lecoq's teaching to be less sophisticated an approach to acting than Stanislavski's script-oriented process – precisely because Lecoq's originates in movement. As recent scholarship shows (e.g. Carnicke, 2002; Kemp, 2012) the linking of Stanislavski with a purely mental and linguistic approach has been overstated, as his "Active Analysis" work demonstrates. Nevertheless, the widespread idea of Stanislavski as "psychological" and Lecoq as "physical" persists, indicated by the tendency of many actor training programmes to teach Stanislavski practice in "Acting" classes and Lecoq work in "movement" classes. This curricular arrangement underestimates the scope and nuance of Lecoq's pedagogy – something that an analysis from the perspective of embodied cognition will show.

The training programme that Lecoq created at his own school drew on many sources, is rooted in physical and verbal improvisation and engages with several theatrical styles – what he called "dramatic territories": Greek Tragedy, Commedia dell'arte, red nose clown, melodrama, the grotesque parodies of "bouffons". Work on these styles is rooted in movement analysis and initial training with the Neutral Mask, created by Lecoq with sculptor and mask-maker Amleto Sartori (1915–1962). The Neutral Mask is a full-face mask, made of leather, with a neutral facial expression. Through wearing it in a variety of exercises and observing others doing the same, actors develop a heightened awareness of the communicative potential of the body. Since we are habituated to pay attention to facial expressions in daily life, the communicative content of posture, gesture and gait becomes much more apparent to the observer when the face is covered – information that can then be used when wearing the mask oneself. The term Neutral Mask refers to the mask itself, the type of exercises conducted with it and the persona that is apparent when a performer wears it. Exercises are always conducted in an ensemble mode, with groups of five to seven students assaying a particular exercise while being observed by the instructor and other students in the larger group of 20 or more. This mode is an important part of the training. Through the process of wearing the mask *and* observing others in it, actors develop many sensitivities, not least an awareness of the communicative potential of the body. Lecoq's use of the mask to train actors is prescient of the discoveries of cognitive science in many ways. For example, a 2005 study demonstrates that bodily posture is highly significant in determining the meaning of emotional facial expressions for observers (Meeren, van Heijnsbergen and de Gelder, 2005). By heightening an actor's awareness and expressive control of postural communication, Lecoq's Neutral Mask exercises assist in clarifying emotional expression when the mask is removed (Lecoq used the Neutral Mask only in training, not for performance). For the wearer of the mask, an interesting phenomenon arises – as one does not need to concern oneself with facial expression as communication, prolonged use of the mask encourages a relaxation of the facial muscles that in turn seems to prompt a sense of calm and focus. Psychologist Paul Ekman's work on facial expressions has shown that consciously arranging the facial musculature in the patterns associated with various primary emotions provokes the affective state of the emotion. This indicates that there is a reflexive proprioceptive relationship between facial musculature and emotion (Ekman, Davidson, & Friesen, 1990, 1999, 2003) – a phenomenon that may explain the sense of calm that arises from the relaxation of the facial muscles under the mask. Other researchers' work point to a similar reflexive (or reciprocal) relationship between larger bodily activity and the experience of emotion (e.g. Duckworth, Bargh, Garcia, & Chaiken, 2002; Stepper & Strack, 1993; Tom, Pettersen, Lau, Burton, & Cook, 1991). Movements of the whole body are involved in Neutral Mask "identifications" work, in which actors consciously embody the rhythms of movement found in natural, social and fabricated environments. This activity forms the foundation of the remarkable synchrony between Lecoq's pedagogy and the precepts of embodied cognition, as it articulates Lecoq's conviction that the starting point for theatre is not a scripted play, but the actor's engagement with the sensorimotor experience of her environment:

> In my method of teaching I have always given priority to the external world over inner experience. . . . It is more important to observe how beings and things move, and how they find a reflection in us. . . . People discover themselves in relation to their grasp of the external world . . . (Lecoq, 2001, p. 19)

This principle of Lecoq's correlates with the foundational concept of embodied cognition that I described earlier; that sensorial and motor experiences form the neural foundations for mental concepts. Beginning with sensorimotor investigations and moving through spoken, then written language, Lecoq's training grounds performance in an explicit re-experiencing of human cognitive development: He states

> [T]he laws of movement govern all theatrical situations. A piece of writing is a structure in motion. Though themes may vary (they belong to the realm of ideas), the structures of acting remain linked to movement and its immutable laws . . . (Lecoq, 2001, p. 24)

Lecoq's idea of "the laws of movement" refers to the affordances and constraints of the typical able-bodied human anatomy and also to the physics of movement in the material environment. His interest in the physics of movement is expressed in the use of architecture as a companion discipline in his school. He and architect Krikor Belekian developed the Laboratoire d'Etude du Mouvement which is taught as a parallel activity to the school's main pedagogy. The course is now lead by Pascale Lecoq who trained as an architect before becoming the school's director.

"Le fonds poetique commun"

As might be expected from Lecoq's statement about the importance of the "external world" much of the content of his training programme arises from his perception of the ways in which humans interact with their material environment. This perception is expressed both in specific exercises and also in broad conceptualisations that create a framework for these exercises. One of the most significant of these conceptualisations is Lecoq's idea of "le fonds poetique commun". A full appreciation of this concept unfortunately requires some reviewing of previous translation. David Bradby, who overall did an admirable job of translating Lecoq's book "Le Corps Poetique" (1997) for its English publication as *The Moving Body* (2001) rendered this phrase as "the universal poetic sense", although he himself has acknowledged in a later editorial comment that "[. . .] the word 'fonds' conveys something more real and concrete than a 'sense'" (Lecoq, 2006, p. xiii). Kemp (2016) has suggested that there is a more nuanced way of understanding this concept than is provided by Bradby's free translation and here I build on that proposal in order to gain a fuller sense of Lecoq's meaning. This is significant, as the concept of "le fonds poetique commun" (properly defined) relates directly to the concept of situated cognition and the sensorimotor links between physical activity and semantic meaning. The association of these features can be drawn out from the way the idea evolved over time in Lecoq's pedagogy and by detailing the semantic associations of the French words that form the phrase.

Lecoq's pedagogy grew organically throughout his life. While "le fonds poetique commun" is a term that he only began to use in last third of his teaching career, practical elements of what he came to define as this concept were present from the inception of his school in 1956. From the beginning, his curriculum incorporated exercises that drew on his own training in sport, as a physical therapist and with French theatre practitioners Jean-Marie Conty and Jean Dasté. These were combined with the results of practical research that he had conducted into the historical styles of Greek tragedy and Commedia dell'arte during an eight-year stint in Italy. As these were both masked styles, they placed emphasis on physical communication in addition to verbal and vocal communication (Commedia used a style of gibberish called *grammlot*). As Lecoq trainee and scholar Ismael Scheffler describes, Lecoq's training incorporated "exercises of movements of identification and expression of natural elements and phenomena" (Scheffler, 2016, p. 182) within its idea of mime (the school's original name was L'École Internationale de Théâtre et de Mime -The International School of Theatre and Mime). It is clear from Lecoq's practices that he used the word mime to suggest physical re-enactment rather than the formalised movement styles associated with Etienne Decroux and Marcel Marceaux. However, while Lecoq's students engaged in activities that consciously mimicked humans' corporeal engagement with the rhythms and sensations of their environment, he struggled to find an explicit way of distinguishing his approach to mime from the stylised and codified approaches of Decroux and Marceau. As Scheffler points out; "Analyzing Lecoq's publications before 1969 ... one can perceive the difficulty Lecoq had until then to define his comprehension of mime" (Scheffler, 2016, p. 182). It was not until Lecoq read the work of anthropologist Marcel Jousse (1886–1961) in the early 1970s that he found both a vocabulary and a conceptualisation that resonated with his own practice. Jousse considered that humans had an unconscious and intuitive ability to reproduce the physical stances, rhythms and movements of beings and objects – a capacity that he called "mimisme" (Jousse, 1932). These ideas enabled Lecoq to refine and articulate what he called his "mimodynamic" approach in which students would first consciously absorb the dynamics of their environment and then "replay" them – a word ("rejeu" in French) that he had adopted from Jousse. By the late 1980s, when Lecoq compiled a book of his own and others' writings that expressed his views on theatre (*Theatre of Movement and Gesture*, 1987), he had assimilated the ideas of Jousse to the point where he quotes him as saying:

> Miming differs from mimicry in this respect; it is not imitation, but a way of grasping the real that is played out in our body. A normal human being is "played" by the reality that reverberates in him. We are the receptacles of interactions that play themselves out spontaneously within us. Human beings think with their whole bodies, they are made up of complexes of gestures and reality is in them, without them, despite them. (Jousse in Lecoq, 2006, p. 9)

Lecoq recapitulated this concept in his own words just a year before his death: "The 'miming body' is the body that has the faculty to take on the dynamics that surround it, the world that surrounds it – like a child. [...] All children are mimes. People [adults] too, but they don't know it" (Lecoq in Roy & Carasso, 1999). The term "mime" with its associations of silent white-gloved performers trapped in glass cases can easily trivialise Lecoq's approach. However his idea of mime has considerable congruity with ideas that influence the field of embodied cognition. Neuropsychologist Merlin Donald proposes that human capacity for symbolic thought arises from three major cognitive evolutions of the brain in symbiosis with culture, with the first being mimesis – a way of representing knowledge through consciously chosen motor activity (1991). Lecoq's concept of mime, shaped by his phenomenological experience imbued with Jousse's analysis, forecasts this understanding:

> Children gain their understanding of the world around them by miming it: they mimic what they see and what they hear. They replay with their whole body those aspects of life in which they will be called on to participate. In this way they learn about life and, little by little, take possession of it. (Lecoq, 2006, p. 1)

It is within the context of these ideas that we need to understand Lecoq's idea of "le fonds poetique commun". As described earlier, Bradby used the term "universal" for the word "commun". Literally translated this would be "common" – in this context meaning "in common" or "shared". The term "fonds commun" is normally translated as "mutual fund" or "common fund". Removed from a financial context, we can understand the use of "fonds" as "fund" in the sense of "fund of knowledge". The word "fonds" also has strong associations of "foundation" or "base" because of its homonym "fond" as in the widely used phrase "au fond"; "at the bottom of". So Lecoq believes that in addition to having principles (or "laws") of movement in common, humans also have a "fund" (or "source") of foundational shared knowledge gained from a mimetic absorption of rhythms and sensorial experience of the physical world. Within this concept, Lecoq's use of the adjective "poetic" is not romantic or vague. His practical investigation of poetry in his pedagogy demonstrates his awareness of the ways in which poetry has effect; the importance of rhythm and sensorial and perceptive stimuli and the centrality of metaphor in human experiencing. (See Gilrain, 2016 for a description of how Lecoq's teaching encourages the conscious awareness of metaphoric thinking to the point of induced kinesthesia). This is significant when we think of Lakoff and Johnson's analysis of metaphor as a fundamental feature of human cognitive activity as physical experience provides the source domain for abstract thought: "Conceptual metaphor is pervasive in both thought and language. It is hard to think of a common subjective experience that is not conventionally conceptualized in terms of metaphor" (Lakoff & Johnson, 1999, p. 45). So "fonds poetique commun" can be understood as a fund of sensorial knowledge that humans have in common developed through physical engagement with the material world. As we can see, this concept accords strongly with the foundational precept of embodied cognition that sensorial and motor experiences form the neural foundations for mental concepts.

Dynamiques

In many of the quotes that I have used, Lecoq uses the term "dynamics" ("dynamiques") to describe the situated environment that humans engage with through physical activity and mimesis. This term is a significant one in his pedagogy as he defines "dynamiques" as combinations of rhythm, force and space. Again, this is an astute conceptualisation when considered through the lens of embodied cognition. The foundational proposition of embodied cognition that I have just reiterated shows us that the mind is inherently embodied, not simply because the brain operates in a body, but because physical experience shapes conceptual thought. Furthermore, thought employs many of the same neuronal pathways as physical action (a process often called "neural exploitation"). Kinesthetic and perceptual experiences of the material world generate cognitive systems that reflect our physical environments and interpersonal experiences and form patterns for higher cognitive activity. As a result, cognitive processes like language and conceptual thought use partial reactivations of sensory, motor and affective systems. As Vittorio Gallese proposes:

> [K]ey aspects of human social cognition are underpinned by brain mechanisms originally evolved for sensorimotor integration. It is proposed that these mechanisms were later on adapted as new neurofunctional architecture for thought and language, while retaining their original functions as well. By neural exploitation, social cognition and language can be linked to the experiential domain of action. (Gallese, 2008: 317)

So for Lecoq to describe lived experiences in the physical world as "dynamics" – combinations of rhythm, force and space – is to understand them at their sensorimotor level – the actional level at which we engage with our environments before we start to consciously reflect on them or describe them in language. It is at this level that his Neutral Mask training re-sensitises actors to the sensorimotor sources of mental concepts.

For example, they work with the dynamics of water in different states (bubbling spring, meandering river, stormy sea), of fire, of air, and also those of materials like paper and cellophane, and of humans experiencing varied physical environments. These activities demand a sustained mental and physical discipline to accurately observe and physically embody different dynamics in ways that make them specific and expressive. For instance, the dynamics of waves in a storm are distinct from those of a bubbling brook. The performer must distinguish how the forces within the varied physical constraints affect the water, and change its rhythm, tempo and directional tendencies. These activities provide the actor with a reinvigorated awareness of the relationship between these rhythmic patterns and the concepts that they generate and shape through the relationship between motor cortex activity, thought and language.

Lecoq extends this process beyond simple physical mimicry by subsequently combining the experiential physical activities with varied modes of linguistically expressed meaning – single words, poems, improvised dramatic narrative. Through these sequences of exercises, the "dynamics" of nature and materials are invested in and correlated with the "dynamics" of communicative expression. Lecoq considers that this training develops lasting patterns of behaviour in the performer: "The main result of this identification work are the traces that remain inscribed in each actor, circuits laid down in the body, through which dramatic emotions also circulate, finding their pathway to expression" (Lecoq, 2001, p. 45) Using consciously articulated patterns of muscular activity, actors develop what is known in theatre parlance as "muscle memory" of movement schema that are linked to concepts and emotions. Using concepts from the neuro – and cognitive sciences we could describe this as a refined awareness of the proprioceptive and interoceptive dimensions of emotion and thought. Lecoq's phrase "circuits laid down in the body' also evokes another primary assumption of embodied cognition – "that any type of recall includes a sensorimotor simulation of the processes involved in the original encoding of the experience" (Koch, Fuchs, Summa, and Mulller 2012, p. 2; referencing Barsalou, Niedenthal, Barbey, & Ruppert, 2003; Niedenthal, 2007).

Actions and language

Another result of Lecoq's training is the specificity of expressive physical action that arises from this level of observational and physical rigour. When engaged with language, this physical precision offers us a view of meaning in interpersonal communication that accords with findings that language and gestural actions are intertwined in communication; as cognitive linguist David McNeill asserts, "gestures are an integral part of language as much as are words, phrases and sentences – gesture and language are one system" (McNeill, 1992, p. 2). Lecoq's work on language and gesture can also be usefully appreciated through Glenberg and Gallese's (2011) action-based theory of language. They point to

> findings that strongly support the existence of mirror neurons in the human motor system and [that] have lead to the notion of a mirror neuron system involving areas in the frontal lobes (notably, Broca's area) and parietal lobes. (Glenberg & Gallese, 2011, p. 8)

The significance here is that Broca's area has traditionally been associated in brain research with speech and language. Glenberg and Gallese (2011) are careful to point out that they consider that both emotion and perception systems are active in language in addition to action systems, but have assimilated data from multiple findings to form a theoretical framework that roots language in action. They state that:

> parietal mirror neurons not only code the goal of an executed/observed motor act, like grasping an object, but they also code the overall action intention [. . .] The "motor vocabulary" of grasping–related neurons, by sequential chaining, reorganizes itself as to map the fulfillment of an action intention. The overall action intention (to eat, to place the food or object) is the goal-state of the ultimate goal-related motor act of the chain. (Glenberg & Gallese, 2011)

This concept of an "action intention" meaning that is definable through motor actions is another concept of embodied cognition that Lecoq's practice both anticipates and illuminates. Earlier work (Kemp, 2012; Murray, 2003) has described Lecoq's analysis of, and work with the action verbs of "push" and "pull". This work arises from Lecoq's recognition that these actions are essential in the mechanics of movement and have extensive metaphorical applications in both verbal and nonverbal communication. To conclude this article I will point out another aspect of Lecoq's work with language that anticipates the view in embodied cognition that culture is one of the factors that is involved in the situated nature of meaning.

In the video *Les deux voyages de Jacques Lecoq* (Roy & Carasso, 1999) Lecoq can be seen teaching part of a lesson on language and gesture. He's working on the action verb "je prends" – normally translated as "I take". In the extract of the lesson that is shown in the video, he has divided a large group of about 20 students into nationality groups and asked each group to define the gesture that expresses this action for them. Each group is given a few minutes to confer and practice (the groups work simultaneously) and is then asked to show the gesture while saying the phrase "I take" in their own language. The first group to show their work is composed of five or six Americans (of mixed gender) who stand in a circle. The gesture that accompanies the phrase is a motion with the hand and arm that reaches directly forward in front of the torso, grasps an imagined item and sharply draws it towards the torso. The movement is sudden and forceful and the phrase "I take" is repeated multiple times. Lecoq is surprised; from his French perspective the American version of "take" is described as "arrache" – "grab". The Americans are followed by a group of four British English speakers (again of mixed gender) who stand in a square formation. They say the phrase "I take" once and make a similar gesture to the Americans – reaching out in front, grasping an imagined item, then pulling the item towards themselves. However, the British version, while also including the action of pulling towards the torso, seems less acquisitive than the American because there is less force, a slower tempo and the vocal expression is considerably softer – a contrast that provokes laughter among the observers and the comment from Lecoq that the gesture is "more diplomatic". The British are followed by a group of three Scandinavian women whose symmetrical gesture involves using both hands to reach out rapidly, grasp and then pull an imagined item smoothly towards the torso. The sustained tempo of the pulling action is in marked contrast to the sudden and rapid action of the American gesture, but is nevertheless decisive in quality. The next example is given by an individual – a woman who is the only speaker of Serbo-Croat in the class – whose gesture involves placing both hands on an imagined item in front of her and then pulling this item with a sustained tempo to the right side of her torso. This lateral movement is significantly different from the pulling action of the three previous groups that drew the "taken" item directly towards the torso. The gesture associated with the Serbo-Croat verb does not bring what is taken to the individual but places it to the side. This prompts Lecoq to comment that the gesture evokes the idea of "putting aside for winter". The final group shown in the video is French – again of mixed gender. Their gesture involves both arms and hands reaching out in front of the torso and then resting on an imagined object. This completes the gesture. Intriguingly for English speakers, for whom the word "take" has connotations of "acquire", the gesture has no activity of pulling the imagined item towards the self. Lecoq seems satisfied that the gesture communicates the meaning of the French phrase "je prends", saying "It's mine [. . .] I have my hand on it, I stay there" as an elaboration of the meaning of the gesture. These five gestures are all prompted by the concept "I take" but have significant differences in what they communicate.

Lecoq's training in the dynamics of movement enables both the clear enaction and description of gesture in terms of direction, force, tempo, tension and so on. This level of specificity highlights the visible nuances of meaning among the different nationality groups. When considered in the context of Glenberg and Gallese's Action-based language theory, one can see that Lecoq's approach identifies how the word "take" – apparently equivalent in meaning when translated linguistically – has different action intentions in different cultures. Differences in force, tempo and degree of suddenness between the American, English and Scandinavian groups make gestures that have the same basic components (grasping something in front of oneself, drawing it towards oneself) evoke different qualitative associations. The similarity of the basic action components may relate to the fact that the English "take" has its etymological roots in "taka" – a word from Old Norse, which is the ancestor of Scandinavian languages. As I hope my description has made clear, both the Serbo-Croat and the French gesture associated with the phrase "I take" suggest not jut qualitative differences, but markedly different action intentions. The two-handed drawing motion to the side of the body enacted with the Serbo-Croat "ja uzimam" evokes connotations of "putting aside" – and we see that the gesture enacted with the French "je prends" has no component of pulling the imagined item towards the self. This suggests that the concept involved in "je prends" is more accurately translated into English as "I take hold of" or "I grasp". The video of Lecoq's lesson gives a concrete demonstration of the culturally situated and embodied nature of the concept of "take" through the visibly different action intentions manifested by the varied gestural patterns of the nationality groups. Further differences might well be observed were the nationality groups engaged in such an exercise further sub-divided by gender.

Conclusion

Graduates of Lecoq's training have achieved success in many ways. They work as actors in multiple styles and as clowns and makers and performers of devised theatre, but also as playwrights, and painters and sculptors and directors of film and theatre. Some of the ways in which Lecoq's techniques are now being used are to teach architecture, to teach English as a foreign language, and as part of the training of doctors at St. Bartholomew's Hospital in London. It seems to me that this extraordinary diversity of application arises because Lecoq's concepts of "Tout bouge", "dynamiques" and "le fonds poetique commun" have shaped his training in ways that are congruent with a core proposition of embodied cognition: that meaning results inter-subjectively from our situated interactions with the world. The exercises that Lecoq has developed clarify and articulate this proposition, enabling conscious eliciting of what is often unconscious behaviour in daily life.

Disclosure statement

No potential conflict of interest was reported by the author.

References

Barsalou, L.W., Niedenthal, P.M., Barbey, A., & Ruppert, J. (2003). Social embodiment. In B. Ross (Ed.), *The psychology of learning and motivation* (Vol. 43, pp. 43–92). San Diego, CA: Academic Press.

Carnicke, S. (2002). *Stanislavsky in focus: An acting master for the twenty-first century*. London: Harwood.

Donald, M. (1991). *Origins of the modern mind: Three stages in the evolution of cultures and cognition*. Cambridge, MA: Harvard University Press.

Duckworth, K., Bargh, J., Garcia, A., & Chaiken, S. (2002, November). The automatic evaluation of novel stimuli. *Psychological Science, 13*(6), 513–519.

Ekman, P., Davidson, R. J., & Friesen, W.V. (1990). Emotional expression and brain physiology II: The Duchenne smile. *The Journal of Personality and Social Psychology, 58*, 342–353.

Ekman, P., Davidson, R. J., & Friesen, W.V. (1999). Basic emotions. In T. Dalgleish & M. Power (Eds.), *Handbook of cognition and emotion* (pp. 46–60). New York, NY: John Wiley.

Ekman, P., Davidson, R. J., & Friesen, W.V. (2003). *Emotions revealed: Recognizing faces and feelings to improve communication and emotional life*. New York: Henry Holt.

Evans, M., & Kemp, R. (Eds.). (2016). *The Routledge companion to Jacques Lecoq*. New York: Routledge.

Gallagher, S. (2006). *How the body shapes the mind*. Oxford: Oxford University Press.

Gallese, V. (2008). Mirror neurons and the social nature of language: The neural exploitation hypothesis. *Social Neuroscience, 3*(3–4), 317–333.

Gallese, V., & Lakoff, G. (2005). The brain's concepts: The role of the sensory-motor system in reason and language. *Cognitive Neuropsychology, 22*(3), 455–479.

Gilrain, J. (2016). The mimo-dynamics of poetry, short story and music: Lecoq on Bartok. In M. Evans, & R. Kemp (Eds.), *The Routledge companion to Jacques Lecoq* (pp. 127–134). New York, NY: Routledge.

Glenberg, A. M., & Gallese, V. (2011). Action-based language: A theory of language acquisition, comprehension, and production. *Cortex, 48*(7), 1–18. Retrieved from 13 May, 2016. doi:10.1016/j.cortex.2011.04.010.

Haggard, P., Rossetti, Y., & Kawato, M. (Eds.). (2007). *Sensorimotor foundations of higher cognition: Attention and performance XXII*. Oxford: Oxford University Press.

Johnson, M. (1987). *The body in the mind*. Chicago, IL: University of Chicago Press.

Johnson, M. (1993). Conceptual metaphors and embodied structures of meaning. *Philosophical Psychology*, 6(4), 413–422.

Jousse, M. (1932). Mimétisme et mimisme. 4ème conférence. École d'Anthropologie. 28 nov. 1932. Le cours de Marcel Jousse. CD-room 1/2. Association Marcel Jousse, 2003.

Kemp, R. (2012). *Embodied acting: What neuroscience tells us about performance*. Abingdon: Routledge.

Kemp, R. (2016). Lecoq, embodied cognition and emotion. In M. Evans, & R. Kemp (Eds.), *The routledge companion to Jacques Lecoq* (pp. 199–207). New York, NY: Routledge.

Koch, S., Fuchs, T., Summa, M., & Mulller, C. (Eds.). (2012). *Body memory, metaphor and movement*. Philadelphia: John Benjamins.

Lakoff, G., & Johnson, M. (1999). *Philosophy in the flesh: The embodied mind and its challenge to Western thought*. New York, NY: Basic Books.

Lecoq, J. (1997). *Le Corps Poetique*. Paris: Editions Actes Sud.

Lecoq, J. (2001). *The moving body*. (D. Bradby, Trans). New York, NY: Routledge.

Lecoq, J. (2006). *Theatre of movement and gesture* (ed. D. Bradby). London: Routledge.

McNeill, D. (1992). *Hand and mind: What gestures reveal about thought*. Chicago, IL: University of Chicago Press.

Meeren, H. K. M., van Heijnsbergen, C. C. R. J., & de Gelder, B. (2005). Rapid perceptual integration of facial expression and emotional body language. *Proceedings of the National Academy of Sciences*, 102, 16518–16523.

Murray, S. (2003). *Lecoq*. London: Routledge.

Niedenthal, P. (2007). Embodying emotion. *Science, 316*(5827), 1002–1005.

Roy, J.-N., & Carasso, J.-G. (1999). *Les deux voyages de Jacques Lecoq*. Paris: La Septe ARTE-On Line production ANRAT.

Scheffler, I. (2016). Laboratory of movement study. In M. Evans, & R. Kemp (Eds.), *The routledge companion to Jacques Lecoq* (pp. 179–186). Abingdon: Routledge.

Stepper, S., & Strack, F. (1993, February). Proprioceptive determinants of emotional and nonemotional feelings. *Journal of Personality and Social Psychology, 64*(2), 211–220.

Tom, G., Pettersen, P., Lau, T., Burton, T., & Cook, J. (1991). The role of overt head movement in the formation of affect. *Basic and Applied Social Psychology, 12*, 281–289.

Varela, F. J., Thompson, E., & Rosch, E. (1991). *The embodied mind: Cognitive science and human experience*. Boston, MA: MIT Press.

Theory, practice and performance

Shaun Gallagher

ABSTRACT

I focus on the enactivist and extended mind approaches to embodied cognition (EC), and specifically on the concepts of body schema, affectivity, distributed cognition and intersubjectivity to show how EC has relevance to questions about expert performance, and to the theory and practice of performing arts.

The notion of embodied cognition (EC) has had an increasing impact not only on our understanding of the mind in cognitive science, but also on our understanding of performance in a variety of fields, including athletics (e.g. Ilundáin-Agurruza, 2016; Sutton & McIlwain, 2015; Sutton, McIlwain, Christensen, & Geeves, 2011) and the performing arts (Cook, 2010; Montero, 2015). In this paper I will briefly review several different theoretical concepts that come under the heading of EC. I will then show how different views of EC have sparked a debate concerning the notion of expert practice. Finally, I will suggest some implications for the study of performance in the context of performing arts.

Theory

Mind–body dualism has a long history in a variety of philosophical traditions. Within such traditions one finds primacy given to ideational/intellectual processes where the body is taken to be irrelevant except for sensory input and motor output. These traditional views carry over into the (1950–1980s) "cognitive revolution", where computational and representational processes "in the head" (mind or brain) are considered to be the only processes that matter for cognition. Challenging this kind of internalism, the notion of the embodied mind started to take shape in the 1990s (e.g. Varela, Thompson, & Rosch, 1991), drawing on phenomenology, and especially the work of Merleau-Ponty. On various views of EC, the body, situated in the surrounding physical and social environment, plays a constitutive role in cognition. Basic cognition and human intersubjectivity are deeply and inextricably embodied, environmentally embedded (situated), closely tied to action and extended (distributed) into the use of tools, technologies and other aspects of the environment. Such views have had an influence, not only in the cognitive sciences, but also in psychiatry and psychological therapy (Gallagher & Payne, 2014; Gallagher & Væver, 2004; Röhricht, Gallagher, Geuter, & Hutto, 2014), and more recently in the humanities, the arts and in studies of performance (Anderson, 2015; Anderson et al., 2015; Høffding, 2015).

In most EC approaches there is general (although not unanimous) agreement opposing internalism – the notion that cognition is entirely "in the head" or a matter of individualistic mechanisms. Beyond that, however, there are philosophical disputes within EC and no overall consensus about some very basic concepts, including the concept of "mental representation".

Consider, for example, the concept of *body schema*, which was central to Merleau-Ponty's (2012) analysis of perception and continues to be of relevance in a variety of fields, including medicine, psychiatry, sports science, etc. The *body schema* is the system of sensory-motor processes that function without necessarily involving perceptual monitoring or awareness. The body schema governs postural and motor control during action, much of which occurs automatically and non-consciously. In learning a new movement, in the context of athletic practice or dance, however, one may start by self-consciously attending to one's posture, balance and limb position as one attempts to move them properly to the task. One's attention might also be directed to such bodily movement by the instructions of a trainer. With practice, however, the formation of motor habits, and with gains in expertise in movement, one's attention is typically directed elsewhere, away from the specifics of bodily movement, and more towards elements of the world, including others. In such cases, practiced body-schematic processes take over and at least some aspects of movement and action become trained or automatic (Pereira, Abreu, & Castro-Caldas, 2013).

On cognitivist models, the body schema is reduced to strictly neuronal processes or body maps in the brain. Berlucchi and Aglioti (2010), for example, look in the brain to identify a specific anatomical and functional neural system responsible for the immediate and automatic guidance of action, centred in the posterior parietal cortex – a body representation equivalent to the body schema. This "body-in-the-brain" strategy, however, runs into problems that derive in part from the complex ambiguities involved when it comes to mapping out brain function (see Gallagher, 2012). Regardless of whether one can isolate a neural representation corresponding to the body schema, however, on the EC, dynamical-embodied conception, body-schematic processes involve extensive peripheral and extra-neural factors, including proprioceptors (which involve both neural and non-neural parts), joints and muscles. Likewise, body-schematic processes are not reducible to simple motor programmes (e.g. Neilson & Neilson, 2005), equivalent to a computational pre-programming of movement that is automatically and inflexibly exercised in a certain behavioural context. Motor responses, for example, rather than fully determined at brain-level, are mediated by the design of muscles and tendons, their degrees of flexibility, their geometric relationships to other muscles and joints, and their prior history of activation. In terms of dynamical systems theory, body-schematic processes involve ongoing adjustments made in response to environmental changes, where parts of the environment can modulate body-schematic processes (Gallagher, 2005a). In addition, however, such motor processes, no matter how automatic, are modulated by the agent's intention. Reaching to pick up an apple may involve many of the same motor processes in different instances, but if one reaches to pick it up in order to take a bite of it, *versus* to offer it to someone, *versus* to throw it, the precise kinematic details of the movements are different (Becchio, Manera, Sartori, Cavallo, & Castiello, 2012).

The body schema begins to form early in fetal development and is functional at birth in a way that may explain phenomena such as early hand–mouth coordination, and the possibility of neonate imitation (Gallagher & Meltzoff, 1996). Even if present at birth it continues to develop, along with body growth and development, throughout childhood. The attunement of the body schema to specialised movements in athletics and other kinds of performance is an important aspect of training and self-training.

Beyond that, it is important to note that the body schema is clearly affected by various cultural and social factors, as pointed out by feminists and race theorists (e.g. Fanon, 2008; Weiss, 2015; Young, 1980). It is also the case that the body schema can expand to include clothes, tools and instruments. Merleau-Ponty (2012), following Head (1920), mentions the case of the blind man's cane. Empirical studies have demonstrated the incorporation of various tools into the body schema (Maravita & Iriki, 2004; Maravita, Spence, Kennett, & Driver, 2002). This is often characterised, in part, as extending the range of peripersonal space to encompass the reach of the tool during use. Tools and instruments, through habitual use, become extensions of one's body, and any modification in the instrument involves a modulation in the body schema. There is also evidence for the formation of a "joint body schema" during a cooperative action scenario; peripersonal space extends to include the reachable space of one's nearby action partner (Soliman, Ferguson, Dexheimer, & Glenberg, 2015; Soliman & Glenberg, 2014).

The idea of a body schema that extends in order to incorporate tools and instruments is consistent with one of the most significant theoretical developments in EC – the notion of distributed cognition, or the "extended mind" (Clark, 2008). According to the extended mind hypothesis the mechanisms (vehicles) of cognition include pieces of the environment – the tools and technologies that we use to accomplish cognitive tasks (e.g. pencil and paper to do math, notebooks or personal digital assistants for memory) – some of which (e.g. prosthetics, cognitive enhancements, etc.), might be incorporated into the body, or the body schema. The extended mind hypothesis develops an idea originally suggested by pragmatist thinkers like John Dewey.

> Hands and feet, apparatus and appliances of all kinds are as much a part of it [thinking] as changes in the brain. Since these physical operations (including the cerebral events) and equipment are a part of thinking, thinking is mental, not because of a peculiar stuff which enters into it or of peculiar non-natural activities which constitute it, but because of what physical acts and appliances do: the distinctive purpose for which they are employed and the distinctive results which they accomplish. (Dewey, 1916, pp. 8–9)

Clark's (2008) conception of the extended mind builds on a functionalist view that downplays the role of the biological body – cognition could be instantiated in a robotic body, for example. Moreover, he considers the notion of representation as important for an explanation of both basic action-oriented behaviour and higher-order, "representation-hungry" cognition. Higher representational processes of the cognitive system will provide "compensatory adjustments" to even out differences in the experiential aspects (caused, for example, by differences in bodily systems) accompanying cognition.

In contrast, enactivist approaches to EC reject the notion of internal, mental representation entirely. Building on the phenomenology of Merleau-Ponty, enactivism emphasises the idea that perception is not just a passive sensory processing of information, it is rather closely connected to action. Perception is action oriented, or "for action", and this action-orientation shapes most cognitive processes. Perception is thus viewed as pragmatic and best explained in terms of body-relative affordances (Gibson, 1977). Affordances are relational insofar as they are constituted, not just by the objective features of the environment, but also by the particular embodiment and skill level of the agent who is coupled with the physical and social environment. Like the extended mind idea – the mind is not simply "in the head" or reducible to brain processes; rather, it is distributed across body and environment, to the extent that body and environment are dynamically coupled. Accordingly, for enactivism, the explanatory unit is brain–body–environment.

Unlike extended mind proponents, however, enactivists claim that biological and affective bodily processes, as well as environmental factors, shape and contribute to the constitution of consciousness and cognition in an irreducible and irreplaceable way – i.e. the human body as a whole is essential for human cognition. Biological aspects of bodily life, including autonomic, peripheral, affective/emotion systems, have a permeating effect on cognition, as do processes of dynamical sensory-motor coupling (body-schematic processes) between organism and environment. For example, hormonal changes – changes in body chemistry – as well as visceral and musculoskeletal processes, can bias perception, memory, attention and decision-making. Regulation of body chemistry is not autonomous from cognitive processes, and vice versa. "Body regulation, survival, and mind are intimately interwoven" (Damasio, 1994, p. 123). Hunger and fatigue, as well as emotion, or affect more generally, can have a significant impact on cognitive processes (e.g. Colombetti, 2013; Danziger, Levav, & Avnaim-Pesso, 2011; Gallagher & Bower, 2014).

Enactivism also emphasises the role of intersubjectivity in regard to action and cognition. The presence of others has been shown to affect perception, behavioural response, affective attunement and judgement (Bayliss, Paul, Cannon, & Tipper, 2006, 2007; Hayes, Paul, Beuger, & Tipper, 2008; Sebanz, Knoblich, & Prinz, 2003). Our primary relations with others involve embodied interactions, starting in early infancy, if not prenatally (Trevarthen, 1979). Even in purely observational cases that involve little or no interaction, our motor systems have been shown to resonate to the actions and emotions of others (Gallese, 2014). Such motor resonance is part of what Merleau-Ponty (2012) calls "intercorporeity". Enactivists interpret this type of resonance, not as an internal neural simulation or representation of the other's actions, but as part of an action-preparatory process to respond to the other agent (Gallagher, 2008).

To summarise, EC theory is still unsettled and a number of central issues are still under debate, including disagreements about representation, how we should view embodiment itself, and the nature of the body–environment coupling. Nonetheless, without having to resolve these issues, one can still ask how EC theories might contribute to our understanding of practice and performance. I note, importantly, however, that this is not a one-way inquiry. That is, studies of practice and performance can inform EC theory, and in fact, may contribute to clarifying some of the issues and perhaps settling some of the debates on the theoretical side.

EC and expert practice

Notions of EC have been useful for defining expertise – and I think this is a good bridge to help us cross over to issues that involve performance in areas such as music and dance. Dreyfus (2005) and Dreyfus and Dreyfus (1980), for example, drawing on ideas from

Merleau-Ponty, defines a set of stages in accomplishing expertise modelled on embodied coping (the body interacting with the environment).

(1) *Novice practitioner* – this stage is characterised by "rigid adherence to taught rules or plans".
(2) *Advanced beginner* – marks improvement over the novice stage, but still lacks any subtle discrimination.
(3) *Competent practitioner* – works with more information and starts to see different applications; such practitioners can plan out a routine.
(4) *Proficient practitioner* – gains a holistic view of situations and prioritises important features; such practitioners can adapt to the situation at hand.
(5) *Expert practitioner* – transcends the rules and has an "intuitive grasp of situations based on deep, tacit understanding".

On Dreyfus's account engagement in embodied practice leads to habit formation where doing becomes automatic, without the necessity of reflection or thought. That is, the expert practitioner, in any realm, from playing tennis, to playing chess, to doing mathematics, does not have to think about what to do – she has an intuitive and automatic insight into how to move or what needs to be done. For Dreyfus, this is so much the case that reflective consciousness of one's doing may in fact disrupt the practice. As Beilock (2010) puts it, "highly practiced skills become automatic, so performance may actually be damaged by introspection, which is characteristic of an earlier, consciously-mediated stage". For Dreyfus (2005), expert performance is mindless, if we understand "mind" in the traditional way. To the extent that the mind is embodied, it is non-representational. Thus, Dreyfus (2002) argues that for practiced or skillful intentional action one does not require representation.

> A phenomenology of skill acquisition confirms that, as one acquires expertise, the acquired know-how is experienced as finer and finer discriminations of situations paired with the appropriate response to each. Maximal grip [a concept discussed by Merleau-Ponty] names the body's tendency to refine its responses so as to bring the current situation closer to an optimal gestalt. Thus, successful learning and action do not require propositional mental representations. They do not require semantically interpretable brain representations either. (2002, p. 367)

Dreyfus associates the idea of representation, and the traditional concept of mind, with a failed Cartesian philosophy – bound up with epistemic states of *knowing-that* (propositional knowledge), when everything about intelligent action and *knowing-how* depends on being-in-the-world (rather than standing back and representing the world) and on context – both background and immediate context. In this regard Dreyfus comes close to the enactivist view of EC. For both Dreyfus and Merleau-Ponty, mind, understood as non-representational embodied mind, is not excluded from movement, but redefined as the expression of an embodied intelligence.

At the same time, Dreyfus over-emphasises the lack of reflection and thought in expert performance. In this respect, he has been subject to a number of critiques based on the study of sport-, dance- and music-performance. John Sutton, for example, taking his direction from sports performance, has proposed what he calls the "AIR" model: "applying intelligence to the reflexes" (Sutton et al., 2011). On this model, expert performance is not without some sort of reflection. A player of cricket, for example, with less than half a second to execute hitting a hard fast ball travelling at 140 km/h, draws not only on smoothly prac-ticed batting, but also on context and conditions relevant to the game, in order to hit a shot with extraordinary precision through a slim gap in the field. "It's fast enough to be a reflex, yet it is perfectly context-sensitive. This kind of context-sensitivity, we suggest, requires some forms of mindedness ... [an] interpenetration of thought and action exemplified in such open skills" (Sutton et al., 2011, p. 80). The expert cricket player is not on automatic pilot – he has trained up his body-schematic control of movement, but what he needs to do in the context of a game is not automatic.

> Skill is not a matter of bypassing explicit thought, to let habitual actions run entirely on their own, but of building and accessing flexible links between knowing and doing. The forms of thinking and remembering which can, in some circumstances, reach in to animate the subtle kinaesthetic mechanisms of skilled performance must themselves be redescribed as active and dynamic. Thought, again, is not an inner realm behind practical skill, but an intrinsic and worldly aspect of our real-time engagement in complex physical and cultural activities .... So expert performers precisely counteract automaticity, because it limits their ability to make specific adjustments on the fly .... Just because skillful action is usually pre-reflective, it does not have to be mindless. (Sutton et al., 2011, p. 95)

Automatic control has limited ability to cope with variability; skill requires the flexibility pro-vided by cognitive processes (Christensen, Sutton, & McIlwain, 2015, 2016). The cognitive processes at stake, however, are not heavy reflective processes, but awareness of the situ-ation and a performative awareness (see below) that mesh with a performative know-how. This is not an awareness of detailed motoric processes (such processes are trained into the body schema), but selective target control for features, such as the goal of the action, or parameters of execution (timing, force, etc.) (Christensen et al., 2016). The consolidation of fine motoric details in body-schematic processes allows for this type of minimal and targeted reflective awareness.

Artistic performance

Montero (2012, 2016) offers a similar critique of Dreyfus, drawing on her own experience as a former professional ballet-dancer. She rejects the idea that expert performance some-how is effortless or thoughtless. She argues that although certain types of bodily awareness may interfere with well-developed skills, it is typically not detrimental to the skills of expert athletes or performing artists. A form of performance thinking is generally better than not thinking. Montero examines a number of scientific studies that purport to show that paying attention to certain bodily aspects of performance will interfere with performance. She con-tends that the studies are not ecological – that is, they introduce types of cognitive efforts that are simply not found in usual practice – e.g. one study asks a player to pay constant attention to his feet as he dribbles a football (e.g. Ford, Hodges, & Williams, 2005). She also cites qualitative studies that indicate that certain types of conscious monitoring (different in different performances) improve performance. Likewise, reports from experts confirm this. Timothy Gallwey, a pro-tennis player observes that:

> when you increase your stroke speed to normal and begin hitting, you may be particularly aware of certain muscles. For instance, when I hit my backhands, I am aware that my shoul-der muscle rather than my forearm is pulling my arm through .... Similarly, on my forehand I am particularly aware of my triceps when my racket is below the ball. (cited in Montero, 2015, p. 135)

How precisely is one conscious of such things? I have argued that it involves a pre-reflective pragmatic self-awareness that does not take the body as an intentional object; a "performative awareness ... that provides a sense that one is moving or doing something, not in terms that are explicitly about body parts, but in terms closer to the goal of the action" (Gallagher, 2005b, p. 73). Legrand (2007), following up on the notion of performative awareness, distinguishes between three types of attention focused on the body:

> *Opaque:* which is thematic, reflective and objectifying, and characterises a novice performance when someone is learning to move in dance or music.

> *Transparent:* when the body is experienced nonthematically, prereflectively and as an aspect of the acting subject – as in everyday walking.

> *Performative:* (as in expert dancers): "A dancer is very concerned with his body and while dancing he is intensively attending to it. But he is not attending to it reflectively as an object. Rather, his awareness of his body as subject is heightened" (Legrand, 2007, p. 512).

Expertise can put this subjective character of experience "at the front" of one's experience without turning experience or action into a mere intentional object (see Toner, Montero, & Moran, 2016).

With respect to musical performance, cellist Ingal Segev emphasises the importance of keeping one's actions in the conscious mind: "my teacher [Bernard Greenhouse], would say, 'don't let the music lead you; you need to direct it'" (cited in Montero, 2015, p. 136). Montero interprets this as follows:

> The idea that you should get lost in the music and simply let it lead you was mistaken, she thinks, as it proscribes thought. If being in the zone for a musical performance means performing at one's best, being in the zone according to Ingal means, it seems, extensive conscious thought about what to do and when to do it. (2015, p. 136)

Montero allows for the possibility that high performers occasionally enter a mindless zone when engaged in optimal performance. She also allows for the possibility that it is generally true that optimal performance coincides with thoughtful performance. This view is reinforced by a recent study of expert music performance by Høffding (2015).

Høffding worked with the Danish String Quartet, conducting phenomenological interviews – interviews that focus on the precise experiences the musicians have while playing their best. Each member of the quartet had different experiences while playing, but all of them reported that they could be thinking of or experiencing different things.

> [...] expert musicians can undergo a wide range of different experiences while playing, from thinking about where to go for beers after the performance, to worrying whether one's facial expression looks interesting to the audience, to enjoying the fact that the playing seems to be unfolding smoothly, and finally to a deep absorption in which one experiences a profound transformation of consciousness. (Høffding, 2015, pp. 11–12)

Høffding (2015, p. 129ff) distinguishes between four different states of awareness in expert performance. The first two are experienced in standard expert playing (where the performer may be thinking of different things).

(1) *Absent-minded playing* (automatic performance; where the body carries on without monitoring).

(2) *Playing under stress* (e.g. after interruption) and striving to get back – "just barely keeping up without missing the notes, yet coping nevertheless, managing to perform without mistakes".

The second two are experienced while playing in deep absorption.

(1) *Blackout*: lack of self-awareness.
(2) *Heightened awareness* of self and surroundings.

The phenomenologically evidenced fact that there are different possible conscious states while engaged in performance goes against Dreyfus's exclusion of awareness or thought. The phenomenological details are telling in this respect. Focusing on deep absorption, Høffding's musicians suggest modulations in the sense of agency: a diminished sense of agency in blackout, and an increased sense of agency in heightened awareness. More precisely, in both states of absorption there is a certain *letting go* that involves *passivity*. Even with increased sense of control in heightened awareness, the performer does not intervene in the process, but lets it happen.

EC in performance: four factors

Høffding's analysis points to four factors that account for the performance being carried along in a way that involves this kind of passivity: body-schematic processes; affect (emotion); the music itself; the other players (Høffding, 2015, p. 177ff). I want to suggest that these factors are not entirely reflective of passivity, but that there is a dynamical interrelation among these factors that also reflect the centrality of bodily action that is involved in the intentionality of the performance itself. I will try to show how these factors are, in some important respects integrated, in ways that play off the first factor, the body schema.

The body schema is attuned by practice so that one can simply play "from the body schema" in a way that allows one to forget about many details of the performance, thereby giving one freedom to focus on selective target control. Members of the quartet report: "You let the body function on its own". "You're surprised about how much the fingers remember themselves. Let the fingers play . . . . Let go and think about something else" (Høffding, 2015, p. 180). As Bowman (2004, p. 44) suggests:

> Developing skillful musical agency entails assuming and assimilating embodied stances, postures, and movements. In becoming skilled musicians, students assimilate the corporeal postures and gestures of teachers – making them their own, weaving them into the dense fabric of their own embodied identity.

Body-schematic attunement alone, however, is not sufficient for expert performance. Affect is also important, and as Høffding suggests, in some cases indicates a difference between musical performance and athletic performance. "With . . . the emotions, *prima facie*, we have reason to differentiate the phenomenology of artistic absorption from athletic absorption" (Høffding, 2015, p. 191). As I understand this claim, Høffding does not think that athletic performance lacks emotion (one only needs to play ice hockey once to understand that emotion plays an important role), but rather that emotion (and the other factors – body schema, the music, intersubjective interactions) work differently in musical performance. In this respect, at least in part, the important differences may have to do with the way that these factors interrelate with each other. With respect to emotion, for example, we may want to distinguish between instrumental action (primarily under body-schematic control), and expressive movement. Aspects of emotion in expressive movement, as found in acting, dance and musical performance, can work like gesture and language in a way that goes beyond simple motor control, but also requires it.[1]

Affect/emotion in relation to music goes in two directions. First, music allows us to explore or develop or regulate emotion in a new way; second, we "offload" some of the power of emotion in the playing of music (Krueger, 2014). If emotion in some cases drives expressive movement during music performance, however, we should not think that it does so independently of the body schema. It is not the case that the body schema carries on independently, delivering technically proficient movement, to which we then add an expressive style motivated by specific emotions relative to the occasion. The expressive style is already integrated into the movement. One could also think that emotion may have its effect directly on body-schematic processes – slowing down or speeding up such processes, for example, or leading to the adoption of certain initial postures that may influence the performance.

The music itself plays an important part in the performance process. We may think of this aspect in terms of the extended mind idea, although music clearly ignores internal *versus* external boundaries. As performers we can get caught up in the music itself. Many studies show that we incorporate tools and instruments into our body schema, or that we extend our body schema into such instruments (e.g. Maravita & Iriki, 2004). On the one hand, therefore, we may think that body-schematic processes add to the music itself as it is generated in the musical instruments. On the other hand, it goes deeper than this: music moves us; it is something that engages the body schema through its links to rhythm, material resonance, muscle, movement and action.

> The sounds of music enter the body and are sensed, felt, and experienced inside the body in a way that, on the whole, the media of other artistic and cultural forms are not. And if one accepts the notion of affordance, then it is not a big step to realizing that there is an element of direct material leverage in the manner in which the sounds of music serve to construct and position individuals in their embodied, everyday lives. (John Shepherd, 2002, cited in Bowman, 2004, p. 40)

Finally, the other players enter the performance. In the context of making music together, Høffding takes music and intersubjectivity to be interrelated. To specify this in a way that Høffding does not, we can explicate this relation in the light of the recent research that shows while working (or playing) together (in joint action) we form "joint body schemas" (Soliman & Glenberg, 2014), and that one's peripersonal space extends to include, not just instruments, but other people we are playing with. Moreover, as we learn from developmental studies, our body-schematic processes and our social interactions may involve what Trevarthen calls intersubjective musicality. Intersubjective musicality is involved in our very first way of communicating – as in infant–caregiver interactions.

> Music moves us because we hear human intentions, thoughts and feelings moving in it, and because we appreciate their urgency and harmony. It excites motives and thoughts that animate our conscious acting … . It appeals to emotions … . Evidently a feeling for music is part of the adaptations of the human species for acting in a human-made world; part, too, of

how cultural symbols and languages are fabricated and learned. (Trevarthen, Delafield-Butt, & Schögler, 2011, p. 12)

Bowman (2004) makes a similar point, contending that this process starts even before birth.

It is important to begin, I think, with the sonorous roots of music and musical significance: with the way the human body is hardwired for sound, and the potential relevance of such phenomenal facts for musical experience. The world of the ear is one we first inhabit three months before birth. Well before we have begun to explore (or create?) the world with our eyes, imparting to it the clarity and objectivity characteristic of visual experience, we experience and interpret our world through the polyvalence of sound. (Bowman, 2004, p. 37)

Conclusion

In these previous paragraphs I have been emphasising a holistic interrelationship between the four factors that Høffding identifies as involved in a kind of performative passivity. If it is difficult to pull apart this passivity ("letting it happen") from the activity of the performance itself, which involves, as suggested by Segev and her teacher Greenhouse, some form of active direction, this simply reflects the dynamical process involved in embodied performance, which in turn depends on an integration that is clearly mapped out in EC accounts of body schematic, affective, extended and intersubjective aspects of perception, action and cognition – all of which are involved in performance.

Note

1. The distinction between instrumental and expressive movement can be seen, for example, in a subject who lacks proprioception and full body-schematic control, and who can accomplish instrumental actions (e.g. picking up a glass) only by alternative use of vision and cognitive effort, but who nonetheless is able to gesture in communicative/expressive action without body schema, vision of gesture or cognitive effort (Cole, Gallagher, & McNeill, 2002).

Disclosure statement

No potential conflict of interest was reported by the author.

Funding

This work was supported by the Australian Research Council grant [DP170102987].

References

Anderson, M. (2015). *The renaissance extended mind*. Berlin: Springer.

Anderson, M., Cairns, D., Czarnecki, B., Garratt, P., Rousseau, G., Sprevak, M., & Wheeler, M. (2015). *History of distributed cognition project*. Edinburgh: Edinburgh University. Retrieved from http://www.hdc.ed.ac.uk/

Bayliss, A. P., Frischen, A., Fenske, M. J., & Tipper, S. P. (2007). Affective evaluations of objects are influenced by observed gaze direction and emotional expression. *Cognition, 104*(3), 644–653.

Bayliss, A. P., Paul, M. A., Cannon, P. R., & Tipper, S. P. (2006). Gaze cuing and affective judgments of objects: I like what you look at. *Psychonomic Bulletin & Review, 13*(6), 1061–1066.

Becchio, C., Manera, V., Sartori, L., Cavallo, A., & Castiello, U. (2012). Grasping intentions: From thought experiments to empirical evidence. *Frontiers in Human Neuroscience, 6*, 1–6.

Beilock, S. (2010). *Choke: What the secrets of the brain reveal about getting it right when you have to*. New York: Simon and Schuster.

Berlucchi, G., & Aglioti, S. M. (2010). The body in the brain revisited. *Experimental Brain Research, 200*, 25–35.

Bowman, Q. (2004). Cognition and the body: Perspectives from music education. In L. Bresler (Ed.), *Knowing bodies, moving minds: Toward embodied teaching and learning* (pp. 29–50). Dordrecht: Kluwer Academic Press.

Christensen, W., Sutton, J., & McIlwain, D. (2015). Putting pressure on theories of choking: Towards an expanded perspective on breakdown in skilled performance. *Phenomenology and the Cognitive Sciences, 14*(2), 253–293.

Christensen, W., Sutton, J., & McIlwain, D. J. (2016). Cognition in skilled action: Meshed control and the varieties of skill experience. *Mind & Language, 31*(1), 37–66.

Clark, A. (2008). *Supersizing the mind: Reflections on embodiment, action, and cognitive extension*. Oxford: Oxford University Press.

Cole, J., Gallagher, S., & McNeill, D. (2002). Gesture following deafferentation: A phenomenologically informed experimental study. *Phenomenology and the Cognitive Sciences, 1*(1), 49–67.

Colombetti, G. (2013). *The feeling body: Affective science meets the enactive mind*. Cambridge: MIT Press.

Cook, A. (2010). *Shakespearean neuroplay: Reinvigorating the study of dramatic texts and performance through cognitive science*. London: Palgrave Macmillan.

Damasio, A. (1994). *Descartes error: Emotion, reason, and the human brain*. New York, NY: G. P. Putnam.

Danziger, S., Levav, J., & Avnaim-Pesso, L. (2011). Extraneous factors in judicial decisions. *Proceedings of the National Academy of Sciences of the United States of America, 108*(17), 6889–6892.

Dewey, J. (1916). *Essays in experimental logic*. Chicago, IL: University of Chicago Press.

Dreyfus, H. L. (2002). Intelligence without representation – Merleau-Ponty's critique of mental representation the relevance of phenomenology to scientific explanation. *Phenomenology and the Cognitive Sciences, 1*(4), 367–383.

Dreyfus, H. L. (2005). Overcoming the myth of the mental: How philosophers can profit from the phenomenology of everyday expertise. *Proceedings and Addresses of the American Philosophical Association, 79*(2), 47–65.

Dreyfus, S. E., & Dreyfus, H. L. (1980). *A five-stage model of the mental activities involved in directed skill acquisition* (No. ORC-80-2). Berkeley Operations Research Center, California University.

Fanon, F. (2008). *Black skin, white masks*. (R. Philcox, Trans.). New York, NY: Grove Press.

Ford, P., Hodges, N. J., & Williams, A. M. (2005). Online attentional-focus manipulations in a soccer dribbling task: Implications for the proceduralization of motor skills. *Journal of Motor Behavior, 37*, 386–394.

Gallagher, S. (2005a). Dynamic models of body schematic processes. In H. De Preester & V. Knockaert (Eds.), *Body image and body schema* (pp. 233–250). Amsterdam: John Benjamins.

Gallagher, S. (2005b). *How the body shapes the mind*. Oxford: Oxford University Press.

Gallagher, S. (2008). Neural simulation and social cognition. In J. A. Pineda (Ed.), *Mirror neuron systems: The role of mirroring processes in social cognition* (pp. 355–371). Totowa, NJ: Humana Press.

Gallagher, S. (2012). The body in social context: Some qualifications on the "warmth and intimacy" of bodily self-consciousness. *Grazer Philosophische Studien, 84*, 91–121.

Gallagher, S., & Bower, M. (2014). Making enactivism even more embodied. *AVANT/Trends in Interdisciplinary Studies (Poland), 5*(2), 232–247.

Gallagher, S., & Meltzoff, A. (1996). The earliest sense of self and others: Merleau-Ponty and recent developmental studies. *Philosophical Psychology, 9*, 211–233.

Gallagher, S., & Payne, H. (2014). The role of embodiment and intersubjectivity in clinical reasoning. *Body, Movement and Dance in Psychotherapy, 10*(1), 68–78. doi:10.1080/17432979.2014.980320

Gallagher, S., & Væver, M. (2004). Disorders of embodiment. In J. Radden (Ed.), *The philosophy of psychiatry: A companion* (pp. 118–132). Oxford: Oxford University Press.

Gallese, V. (2014). Bodily selves in relation: Embodied simulation as second-person perspective on intersubjectivity. *Philosophical Transactions of the Royal Society B, 369*(177), 1–10.

Gibson, J. J. (1977). The theory of affordances. In R. Shaw & J. Bransford (Eds.), *Perceiving, acting, and knowing* (pp. 67–82). Hillsdale, NJ: Lawrence Erlbaum.

Hayes, A. E., Paul, M. A., Beuger, B., & Tipper, S. P. (2008). Self produced and observed actions influence emotion: The roles of action fluency and eye gaze. *Psychological Research, 72*(4), 461–472.

Head, H. (1920). *Studies in neurology* (Vol. 2). London: Oxford University Press.

Høffding, S. (2015). *A phenomenology of expert musicianship* (PhD thesis). Department of Philosophy, University of Copenhagen, Copenhagen.

Ilundáin-Agurruza, J. (2016). *Holism and the cultivation of excellence in sports and performance.* London: Routledge.

Krueger, J. (2014). Affordances and the musically extended mind. *Frontiers in Psychology, 4,* 1003. https://doi.org/10.3389/fpsyg.2013.01003

Legrand, D. P. M. (2007). Pre-reflective selfconsciousness: On being bodily in the world. *Janus Head, 9,* 493–519.

Maravita, A., & Iriki, A. (2004). Tools for the body (schema). *Trends in Cognitive Sciences, 8*(2), 79–86.

Maravita, A., Spence, C., Kennett, S., & Driver, J. (2002). Tool-use changes multimodal spatial interactions between vision and touch in normal humans. *Cognition, 83*(2), B25–B34.

Merleau-Ponty, M. (2012). *Phenomenology of perception.* (D. A. Landes, Trans.). London: Routledge.

Montero, B. (2012). Practice makes perfect: The effect of dance training on the aesthetic judge. *Phenomenology and the Cognitive Sciences, 11*(1), 59–68.

Montero, B. G. (2015). Thinking in the zone: The expert mind in action. *The Southern Journal of Philosophy, 53*(S1), 126–140.

Montero, B. G. (2016). *Thought in action: Expertise and the conscious mind.* Oxford: Oxford University Press.

Neilson, P. D., & Neilson, M. (2005). An overview of adaptive model theory: Solving the problems of redundancy, resources, and nonlinear interactions in human movement control. *Journal of Neural Engineering, 2,* S279–S312.

Pereira, T., Abreu, A. M., & Castro-Caldas, A. (2013). Understanding task- and expertise-specific motor acquisition and motor memory formation and consolidation. *Perceptual & Motor Skills, 117*(1), 1150–1171.

Röhricht, F., Gallagher, S., Geuter, U., & Hutto, D. D. (2014). Embodied cognition and body psychotherapy: The construction of new therapeutic environments. *Sensoria: A Journal of Mind, Brain & Culture, 10,* 11–20.

Sebanz, N., Knoblich, G., & Prinz, W. (2003). Representing others' actions: Just like one's own? *Cognition, 88,* B11–B21.

Soliman, T. M., Ferguson, R., Dexheimer, M. S., & Glenberg, A. M. (2015). Consequences of joint action: Entanglement with your partner. *Journal of Experimental Psychology: General, 144*(4), 873–888.

Soliman, T. M., & Glenberg, A. M. (2014). The embodiment of culture. In L. Shapiro (Ed.), *The Routledge handbook of embodied cognition* (pp. 207–220). London: Routledge.

Sutton, J., & McIlwain, D. J. (2015). Breadth and depth of knowledge in expert versus novice athletes. In J. Baker & D. Farrow (Eds.), *The Routledge handbook of sports expertise* (pp. 95–105). London: Routledge.

Sutton, J., McIlwain, D., Christensen, W., & Geeves, A. (2011). Applying intelligence to the reflexes: Embodied skills and habits between Dreyfus and Descartes. *Journal of the British Society for Phenomenology, 42*(1), 78–103.

Toner, J., Montero, B. G., & Moran, A. (2016). Reflective and prereflective bodily awareness in skilled action. *Psychology of Consciousness: Theory, Research, and Practice.* Retrieved from http://dx.doi.org/10.1037/cns0000090

Trevarthen, C. B. (1979). Communication and cooperation in early infancy: A description of primary intersubjectivity. In M. Bullowa (Ed.), *Before speech* (pp. 321–348). Cambridge, MA: Cambridge University Press.

Trevarthen, C., Delafield-Butt, J., & Schögler, B. (2011). Psychobiology of musical gesture: Innate rhythm, harmony and melody in movements of narration. In A. Gritten & E. Kind (Eds.), *New perspectives on music and gesture* (pp. 11–44). London: Routledge.

Varela, F. J., Thompson, E., & Rosch, E. (1991). *The embodied mind: Cognitive science and human experience.* Cambridge: MIT Press.

Weiss, G. (2015). The normal, the natural, and the normative: A Merleau-Pontian legacy to feminist theory, critical race theory, and disability studies. *Continental Philosophy Review*, 48, 77–93.

Young, I. M. (1980). Throwing like a girl: A phenomenology of feminine body comportment motility and spatiality. *Human Studies*, 3(1), 137–156.

Index

INDEX

INDEX

Printed and bound by CPI Group (UK) Ltd, Croydon, CR0 4YY
01/11/2024
01782600-0003